FOOD SAFETY

Because most kids do not have acc~~~~ ~~~~~~
or microwaves at school, take extra care to
ensure their lunches stay out of the temperature
"danger zone." Food-borne bacteria grows
rapidly between 40°F and 140°F (4°C and 60°C).
Foods that remain in this temperature range for
more than two hours could be unsafe to eat.

Invest in some good insulated containers,
and make sure the food is at a good
temperature when it goes in. For hot foods,
pour hot water into the insulated container
and let it sit for a few minutes with the lid on
before adding the food. This will help the
container stay hotter longer. Heat foods just
before you leave the house (or as close as
possible) to minimize the length of time they will be sitting out of
the fridge. Use an instant-read thermometer to make sure they reach
a temperature higher than 140°F (60°C) before putting them in the
container to allow for some cooling.

Pack cold foods into their insulated
containers the night before, if
possible, so the container will be nice
and cool. If you are packing the lunch
up in the morning, fill the container

with cold water (with ice if that is convenient) and place it in the fridge
for 5 to 10 minutes to chill before adding the food. Add cooler packs to
the lunch kit to keep the food below 40°F (4°C).

If perishable items do come back home, don't be tempted to put them
back in the fridge for another day. Even with thermoses to keep things
warm or ice packs to keep them cool, after that many hours with no
refrigeration, the food has probably been in the "danger zone" for
too long to be safe to eat. Your best bet is to just grit your
teeth and throw it out.

Just Eat It!

Which brings us to the other main challenge that can make lunch preparation for kids such a thankless task. Getting them to actually eat it. At the end of the workday, you dig through your kid's bag to fish out the dirty containers so you can wash them for the next day's lunch only to find they are still full. The food you so lovingly packed this morning has returned untouched.

Muttering to yourself as you empty the containers into the garbage, you gloomily wonder, "Why do I even bother?" We get it. This scenario might not be the most frustrating experience of your day, but it's certainly

high on the list, especially when it is a common occurrence. So much food wasted.

As tempting as it may be, though, not bothering is not an option. Kids who are hungry at school are often unable to focus on their lessons and do poorly in the classroom. A hungry kid is a scattered kid; it's hard to concentrate when your tummy is rumbling. Remember, you are not only nourishing their bodies with the lunch you pack, you are also feeding their brains. A nutritious lunch is obviously key to helping kids grow healthy and strong. However, it also allows them to concentrate during class, gives them enough energy to get through the day and helps regulate their mood so they are not little balls of moodiness or rage when you see them after school.

Once you've packed your kid's lunch into their backpack, what happens to it is out of your hands. You have no control over whether or not they eat it or if they trade it with one of their classmates. But there are a few things you can do to stack the odds in your favour.

- **Get your kids involved.** Let them help you prepare and pack the foods that are going into their lunch kit, and give them a say in what they'll be eating. Ask for their opinion and give them choices. This could even extend to taking them on your next shopping trip. Let them pick out some fruit, veggies and such they want for the week. They can't complain about what's in their lunch kit if they helped put it there, and they are more likely to eat foods that they have chosen.

- **Pack things separately to keep them fresh.** For example, for taco salad, store the lettuce in one container and the meat mixture in another so the warm meat doesn't wilt the lettuce.

- **Try your version of a "Bento Box."** These are fun for kids and can't be beat for practicality. Having a container with separate compartments for different foods takes up less room in your child's school bag and reduces the amount of packaging you'll use. Good for your pocketbook and the environment.

- **Include a little freezer pack.** Add a small, frozen, reusable container of water to the lunch kit. It will thaw in time for lunch and keep the surrounding food cool. Juice boxes can also be frozen for the same purpose but are not as good for the environment.

- **Use smaller portions for smaller kids.** A whole apple can be intimidating for a young child and will likely return uneaten or with only a few bites missing. The same apple cut into slices is more likely to disappear. Keep your child's appetite in mind when packing, and include only half the apple, if need be.

- **Toss in a container of dip.** It is amazing what kids will devour if they have a dip to dunk it in.

- **Make food fun!** The saying "You eat with your eyes" exists for a reason. Kids are more likely to be excited about food that is fun and appealing (see p. 10 for ideas).

- **Choose familiar foods.** The lunch box is not the place to introduce new foods. It can take a few tries for a kid to accept a food they have never tried before, and realistically, food that has been sitting in a lunch kit all morning is not at its best. If you give your kids a new food they don't like or don't want to try, the food will be wasted and your kids will be hungry the for rest of the day. New dishes are best introduced at a family meal when your child can see other family members trying and hopefully enjoying the meal.

- **Don't forget cutlery!** Inexpensive reusable cutlery options abound and are widely available. If you are having trouble tracking some down, check camping or outdoor stores. Disposable cutlery is often made from cheap plastic that can crack easily, leaving sharp edges. And it's bad for the environment.

- **Add a cheery note or joke.** A little note, sticker, cute-shaped eraser or other small item added to the lunch kit can really brighten your child's day. Even older kids will enjoy getting a small note or joke that lets them know you are thinking about them.

MAKING FOOD FUN!

Kids eat with their eyes first, so make their lunches fun! It takes only a little extra time and yet reaps so many rewards. Your kids will love it, you'll look like parent of the year and your kids will actually eat their lunch! Use your imagination and have fun with it. Here are a few ideas to help you get started:

• Use cookie cutters to cut things, such as sandwiches, cheese or firm fruit—apples, melon, kiwi, pineapple—into fun shapes.

• Pick a theme and tailor the foods to fit the theme. This works great for special occasions, such as Halloween or Christmas, but can also be an everyday theme, such as spring, your child's favourite animal, etc.

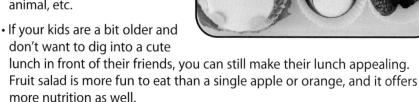

• If your kids are a bit older and don't want to dig into a cute lunch in front of their friends, you can still make their lunch appealing. Fruit salad is more fun to eat than a single apple or orange, and it offers more nutrition as well.

• Kids of all ages love DIY lunches. Make your own homemade versions of the popular commercially available lunch snack kits using nutritious, whole foods instead of highly processed ingredients.

HEALTHY SNACKS FOR GRAZERS

Not every kid wants a "main" for lunch. Some kids appreciate that thermos of chili or a filling wrap, but some kids are grazers. They prefer to eat small snacks more often, or they are too distracted during lunchtime to finish an entire meal.

Rather than packing a main that won't get eaten (or eat least not finished), try packing an assortment of healthy, fun snacks instead. Stay away from highly processed snack foods available on grocery store shelves and whip up a few of the ideas offered below.

- Spread celery sticks with peanut butter or another nut butter and sprinkle raisins on top. Cream cheese also works well.

- Slice red, yellow or orange pepper into "boats" and stuff them with feta cheese

- Cut the top and bottom off an apple, and then cut it horizontally into 4 slices. Remove the core and spread nut butter over 2 slices. If you are feeling fancy, sprinkle granola, coconut or dried cranberries over the nut butter, then top with the remaining 2 slices to make apple "sandwiches." Rub the cut sides of the apple with lemon juice or sprinkle them with cinnamon to prevent browning.

- Freeze a smoothie ahead of time and pack it in the lunch kit. By the time lunch rolls around, the smoothie will have thawed enough to drink, and it will keep the other snacks in the lunchbox cold all morning.

- Make fruit and cheese bites or skewers using your child's favourite fruit and cheeses. You can even roll up some deli meat and add it to a skewer with squares of cheese.

Lunch doesn't have to be complicated. Be flexible. A good lunch is one that contains nutritious foods your kids will actually eat. That nutritionally balanced, whole-food masterpiece of a lunch you created isn't doing anyone any good if it remains untouched.

If your son wants nothing but crackers and cheese for lunch, give him crackers and cheese, just make sure the crackers are whole grain and the cheese is the most nutritious you can buy, rather than a highly processed cheese product. And throw in a sliced apple for good measure. Apples and cheese taste great together!

Chili

Having a batch of this chili on hand opens up a world of lunchtime possibilities. Eat it as-is with some cornbread or a fresh bun on the side, slap it on a hot dog, make your own sloppy joes, use it as a dip or spoon it on a bed of lettuce and add some cheese and tortillas chips for a quick taco salad. The chili will keep in the fridge for about 5 days and can be frozen for up to 3 months.

Cooking oil	2 tsp.	10 mL
Lean ground beef	2 lbs.	900 g
Chopped onion	1 1/2 cups	375 mL
Thinly sliced celery	1 cup	250 mL
Can of tomato sauce (14 oz., 398 mL)	1	1
Barbecue sauce	2 tbsp.	30 mL
Worcestershire sauce	2 tsp.	10 mL
Salt, to taste		
Pepper, to taste		

Heat cooking oil in a large frying pan on medium. Add ground beef and scramble-fry for 5 to 10 minutes until no longer pink. Drain.

Add onion and celery and cook for 10 minutes, until onion is softened.

Add next 5 ingredients and bring to a boil. Reduce heat to a simmer and cook, stirring occasionally, for about 30 minutes. Makes 5 cups (1.25 L).

Chili Sloppy Joes, p. 24

Persian Beef Kabobs

These kabobs can be prepared on an indoor grill if you don't want to fire up the barbecue. They will keep in the refrigerator for 3 to 4 days or in the freezer for up to 2 months. To freeze, arrange the kabobs in a single layer on a baking tray and place it in the freezer until the kabobs are frozen, then transfer them to a resealable freezer bag or airtight container.

Medium onion, grated	1 1/2 cups	375 mL
Lean ground beef	1 1/2 lbs.	680 g
Garlic clove, minced	1	1
Bread crumbs	1 cup	250 mL
Large egg, lightly beaten	1	1
Turmeric	1/2 tsp.	2 mL
Salt	1/2 tsp.	2 mL
Pepper	1/4 tsp.	1 mL

Place onion in a strainer and squeeze out all liquid. Discard liquid.

In a large mixing bowl, combine beef, onion and remaining 6 ingredients. Mix well. Divide beef mixture into 12 portions and shape into 5 inch (12.5 cm) cylinders around 8 inch (20 cm) skewers. Grill on medium-high heat for 7 to 8 minutes, turning occasionally, until cooked through. Allow skewers to cool slightly before removing kabobs. Makes 12 kabobs.

Sliders, p. 26

Meatballs

These meatballs are simple to prepare and so convenient to have on hand when you need a last-minute lunch idea. They can be stored in the fridge for 3 to 4 days or in the freezer for up to 3 months. To freeze, arrange the meatballs in a single layer on a baking sheet and freeze for at least 2 hours. When they are frozen through, transfer the meatballs to a resealable freezer bag or airtight container.

Large egg	1	1
Crushed seasoned croutons	1/4 cup	60 mL
Chopped fresh parsley	2 tbsp.	30 mL
(or 1 1/2 tsp., 7 mL, flakes)		
Grated Parmesan cheese	2 tbsp.	30 mL
Garlic clove, minced	1	1
(or 1/4 tsp., 1 mL, powder)		
Lean ground beef	1 lb.	454 g

Combine first 5 ingredients in a medium bowl.

Add ground beef and mix well. Roll into 3/4 inch (2 cm) balls and arrange on a greased baking sheet with sides. Bake in 350°F (175°C) oven for about 15 minutes until no longer pink inside. Transfer to paper towels to drain. Makes about 65 meatballs.

Mini Meatball Subs, p. 30

Breakfast Sausages

These homemade breakfast sausage patties have a mild maple sweetness that kids will love. They will keep for 3 to 4 days in the fridge or up to 3 months in the freezer. Make sure you freeze the patties individually on baking sheets before transferring them to a resealable freezer bag or airtight container, or they will stick together and you will have trouble prying them apart.

Thinly sliced green onion	1/2 cup	125 mL
Fine dry bread crumbs	6 tbsp.	90 mL
Chopped fresh parsley (or 1 tbsp., 15 mL, flakes)	1/4 cup	60 mL
Maple syrup	4 tsp.	20 mL
Salt	1/2 tsp.	2 mL
Pepper	1/2 tsp.	2 mL
Lean ground pork	2 lb.	900 g
Cooking oil	1 tsp.	5 mL

Combine first 6 ingredients in a medium bowl.

Add ground pork and mix well. Shape into 2 1/2 inch (6.4 cm) diameter patties, using about 1/4 cup (60 mL) for each.

Heat cooking oil in a large frying pan on medium. Add patties and cook for about 5 minutes per side until no longer pink inside. Makes 16 patties.

Omelette Cups, p. 70

Marinated Chicken Strips

These chicken strips can be frozen in the marinade and then thawed and cooked when you need them, or you can cook them before tossing them in the freezer. Cooked chicken strips will keep in the fridge for about 4 days and can be frozen for up to 3 months. To freeze, spread the chicken out on a baking sheet in a single layer and place in the freezer until solid. Transfer the frozen strips to a resealable freezer bag or airtight container.

Boneless, skinless chicken breast	1 1/2 lbs.	680 g
Garlic cloves, minced	1	1
Brown sugar	1 tsp.	5 mL
Lime juice	1 tbsp.	15 mL
Cooking oil	2 tsp.	10 mL

Cut chicken across the grain into strips 1/8 inch (3 mm) thick. Place in a large resealable freezer bag.

Combine remaining 3 ingredients in a small bowl. Transfer mixture to freezer bag. Squeeze air out of bag and seal. Gently squeeze bag to distribute flavours. Marinate in refrigerator for 30 minutes up to 3 hours.

Heat 1 tsp. (5 mL) cooking oil in a large frying pan on medium. Add half of chicken and cook, stirring often, until chicken is golden and cooked though. Repeat with remaining oil and chicken. Makes 4 cups (1 L).

Chicken Fajitas, p. 32

Falafel

These tasty patties are another life-saver when you need a quick, hassle-free lunch idea. Slap them in pita with some fresh veggies, serve them on a bed of greens or pair them with side of dip and you have a quick, delicious meal. The patties can be stored in the fridge for up to 5 days or in the freezer for up to 2 months. To reheat, pan fry or heat in a 375°F (190°C) oven or toaster oven for 10 to 12 minutes if frozen or about 5 minutes if thawed, flipping halfway through the cooking time. You can also make them into balls instead of patties, if you prefer.

Can of chickpeas (19 oz., 540 mL)	1	1
Cooked long grain brown rice	1 cup	250 mL
Tahini	1/2 cup	125 mL
Garlic cloves, minced	2	2
Dried mint	1 tbsp.	15 mL
Ground cumin	1/2 tsp.	2 mL
Salt	1/4 tsp.	1 mL
Pepper	1/4 tsp.	1 mL
Olive oil	3 tbsp.	45 mL

Process first 8 ingredients in a food processor until combined but not completely smooth. Using about 2 tbsp. (30 mL) of mixture, form into balls and flatten into patties about 1/2 inch (12 mm) thick.

Heat 1 tbsp. (15 mL) oil in a large frying pan on medium heat. Cook 6 patties for about 4 minutes per side until golden and heated through. Repeat with remaining oil and patties, wiping pan with paper towel between batches. Makes 18 patties.

Falafel Pita Pockets, p. 34

Roasted Veggies

There is almost limitless possible uses for these versatile veggies: toss them into your pasta or rice dish, add them to a sandwich, use them to top a burger, or sprinkle them into your omelette. They will keep in the fridge for up to 5 days, but do not freeze them as they do not reheat well once frozen.

Olive oil	1/4 cup	60 mL
Fresh rosemary, chopped	1 tbsp.	15 mL
Fresh oregano, chopped	1 tbsp.	15 mL
Salt	1/2 tsp.	2 mL
Pepper	1/4 tsp.	1 mL
Zucchini, cut into 2 inch, 5 cm, strips	2 cups	500 mL
Butternut squash, cut into 2 inch, 5 cm, strips	2 cups	500 mL
Red onion, thinly sliced	2 cups	500 mL
Red pepper, cut into strips	2 cups	500 mL
Yellow pepper, cut into strips	2 cups	500 mL

Combine first 5 ingredients in a large bowl.

Add next 5 ingredients and toss until vegetables are well coated. Spread in a greased 9 x 13 inch (23 x 33 cm) baking dish. Bake, uncovered, in 350°F (175°C) oven for about 75 minutes, stirring occasionally, until butternut squash is tender. Makes 8 cups (2 L).

Roasted Veggie Wrap, p. 98

Oven Omelette

This recipe is a great way to make many omelettes at once, or to make enough to last for a number of days. They will keep in the fridge for 3 to 4 days and can even be frozen for up to 3 months. When portioned individually, they are the perfect size for homemade breakfast sandwiches!

Large eggs	12	12
Cream cheese, softened and cut up	4 oz.	113 g
Milk	1/2 cup	125 mL
Salt	1/4 tsp.	1 mL
Pepper	1/8 tsp.	0.5 mL

Process all 5 ingredients in a blender or food processor until smooth. Pour into a greased 2 quart (2 L) shallow baking dish. Bake, uncovered, in 375°F (190°C) oven for 15 minutes. Stir. Bake for another 10 to 15 minutes until set. Makes 6 servings.

Brunch 'wich, p. 86

French Toast

Baking your French toast makes for a simple solution when you are batch cooking. This recipe can easily be doubled or tripled depending upon how many servings you want to make. Using thick bread slices keeps this French toast moist on the inside, while the exterior is perfectly golden. Store in the fridge 3 to 4 days or in the freezer for up to 2 months.

Large eggs	5	5
Vanilla yogurt	1/2 cup	125 mL
Granulated sugar	3 tbsp.	45 mL
Vanilla extract	1 tsp.	5 mL
Salt	1/2 tsp.	2 mL
Ground cinnamon	1/4 tsp.	1 mL
Texas bread slices	8	8

Whisk first 6 ingredients in a medium bowl until smooth.

Dip bread slices into egg mixture. Place on a greased 11 x 17 inch (28 x 43 cm) baking sheet with sides. Pour any remaining egg mixture over bread slices. Let stand for 5 minutes. Bake in 350°F (175°C) oven for 20 minutes, turning at halftime, until set and edges are golden. Makes 8 toasts.

French Toast Sticks with Maple Yogurt Dip, p. 62

Waffles

These waffles are light and fluffy thanks to the beaten egg whites that are folded into the batter. For a savoury, cheesy version, add 3/4 cup (175 mL) Cheddar cheese and 2 tbsp. (30 mL) green onion to the batter. These waffles will keep in the fridge for 3 or 4 days, but they also freeze wonderfully and can be reheated from a frozen state. For best results, reheat them in a toaster, toaster oven or oven until heated through.

All-purpose flour	1 1/2 cups	375 mL
Granulated sugar	2 tbsp.	30 mL
Baking powder	1 tbsp.	15 mL
Salt	1/2 tsp.	2 mL
Egg whites (large), room temperature	2	2
Egg yolks (large)	2	2
Butter (or hard margarine), melted	1/4 cup	60 mL
Milk	1 1/2 cups	375 mL

Stir first 4 ingredients together in a medium bowl. Make a well in centre.

Beat egg whites in a small bowl until stiff.

Using same beaters, beat egg yolks in a separate bowl. Mix in butter and milk and pour mixture into well. Beat to combine. Fold in beaten egg whites. Cook in hot waffle iron until browned, using about 1/3 cup (75 mL) batter for each. Makes 12 waffles.

Charoset with Waffle Sticks, p. 64

DIY Tacos

What kid doesn't love tacos? We've used round tortilla chips in place of the traditional taco shells, but feel free to pack whatever your child likes best. Make the meat mixture ahead, then reheat it in the microwave and pack it in an insulated container to keep it warm. Let your child choose a selection of their favourite taco fixin's, and pack them in separate containers to keep everything fresh until lunchtime.

Extra-lean ground beef	1 lb.	454 g
Cooking oil	1 tbsp.	15 mL
Chili powder	1 1/2 tsp.	7 mL
Salt	1/2 tsp.	2 mL
Pepper, to taste		
Dried oregano	1/4 tsp.	1 mL
Garlic powder	1/4 tsp.	1 mL
Paprika	1 tsp.	5 mL

Round tortilla chips
Grated medium Cheddar or Monterey Jack cheese
Shredded lettuce
Diced tomatoes
Salsa
Guacamole
Kernel corn

Scramble-fry beef in cooking oil until browned. Drain and stir in next 6 ingredients. Makes about 3 cups (750 mL).

Packing the lunch kit: Reheat a portion of beef mixture in microwave until heated through. Transfer to a warmed insulated container. Pack fixin's in separate containers in an insulated lunch bag with a cooler pack to keep them cool. Pack tortilla chips in a separate container. Makes 1 serving.

At lunchtime, top tortilla chips with beef mixture and sprinkle with fixin's.

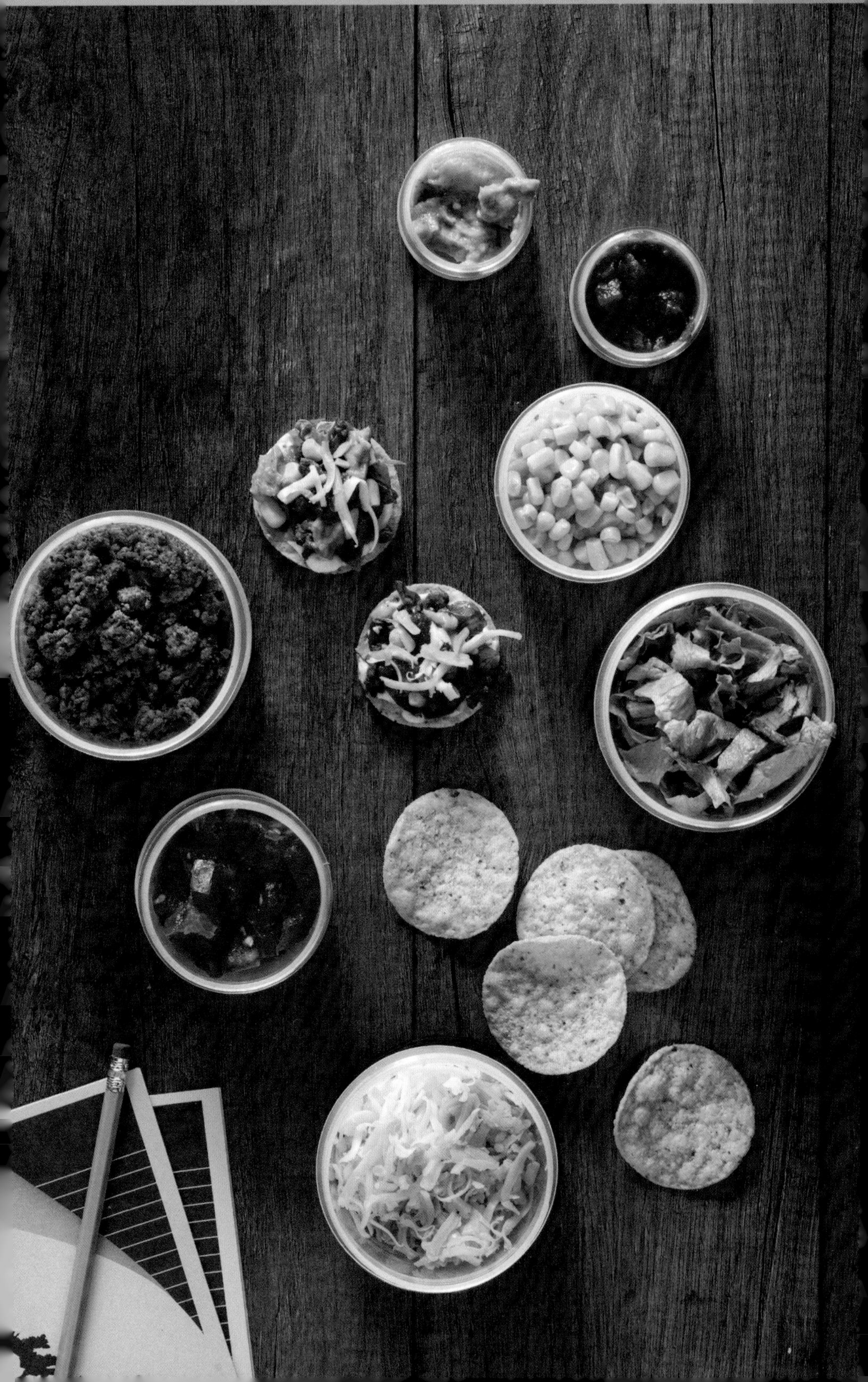

Chili Sloppy Joes

To make these sloppy joes even more fun, we've replaced the standard bun with homemade cornmeal biscuits! This recipe comes together quickly if you use the batch-cooking Chili recipe (see p. 12) The biscuits can be made ahead and stored in an airtight container for about 3 days. They also freeze well but might be a little crumblier once they thaw.

All-purpose flour	1 1/2 cups	375 mL
Yellow cornmeal	1 cup	250 mL
Granulated sugar	1/2 cup	125 mL
Baking powder	2 tsp.	10 mL
Baking soda	1 tsp.	5 mL
Salt	1/2 tsp.	2 mL
Large egg	1	1
Buttermilk (or soured milk, see Tip, below)	1 cup	250 mL
Butter (or hard margarine), melted	1/4 cup	60 mL

Chili (see p. 12)

For the biscuits, combine first 6 ingredients in a large bowl. Make a well in centre.

Combine next 3 ingredients in a small bowl. Add to well. Stir until just moistened. Fill 12 greased muffin cups 3/4 full. Bake in 375°F (190°C) oven for about 15 minutes until wooden pick inserted in centre of muffin comes out clean. Let stand in pan for 5 minutes before removing to a wire rack to cool. Makes 12 muffins.

Packing the lunch kit: Reheat a portion of chili in the microwave or in a pot on the stove until heated through. Transfer to a warmed insulated container. Cut a biscuit in half and place in an airtight container. Makes 1 sloppy joe.

At lunchtime, pour or spoon chili onto bottom half of biscuit. Top with other half of biscuit and enjoy.

Tip: To make soured milk, measure 1 tsp. (5 mL) white vinegar or lemon juice into a 1 cup (250 mL) liquid measure. Add enough milk to make 1 cup (250 mL). Stir well and let sit for 1 minute.

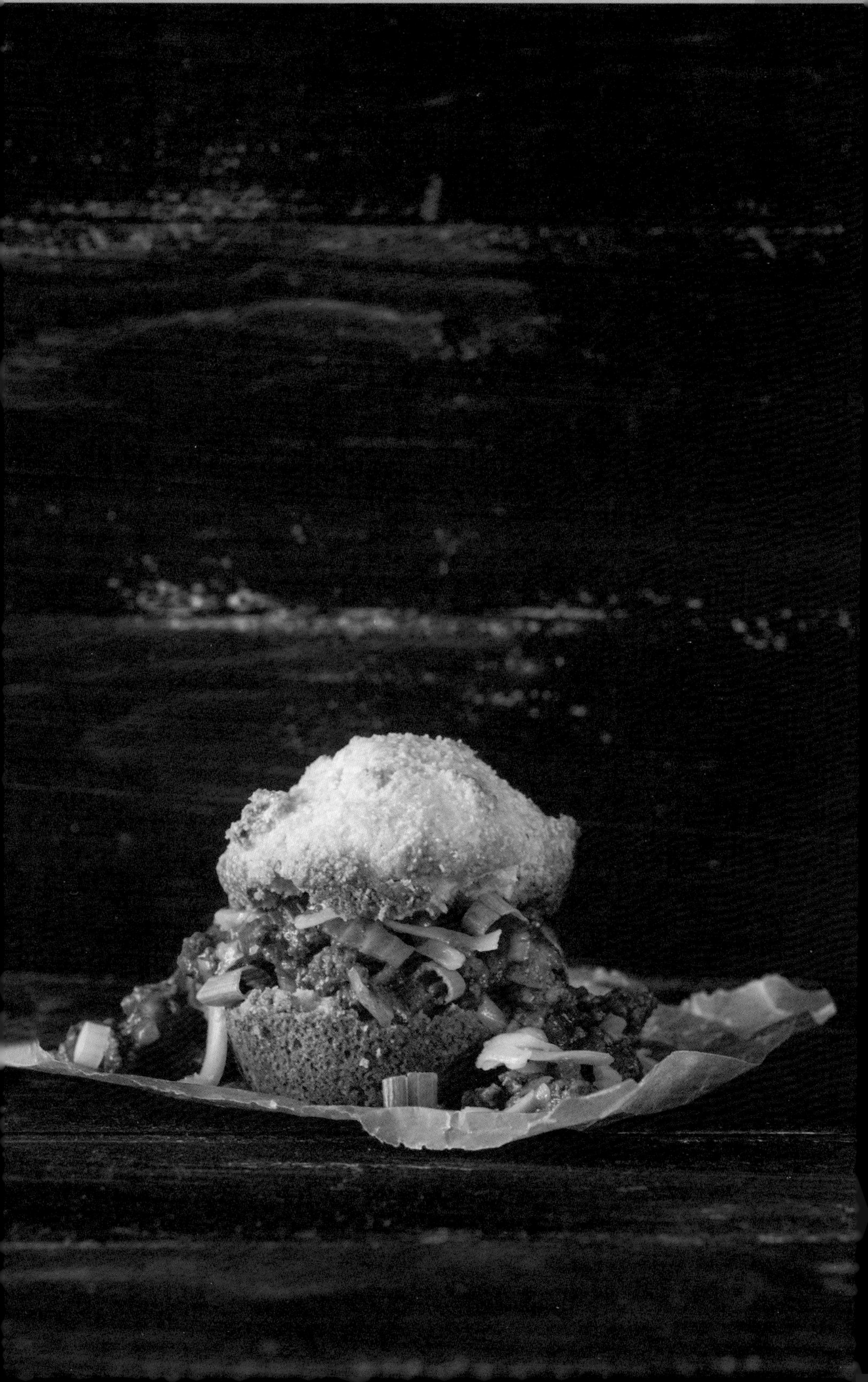

Sliders

Folks with little hands appreciate little burgers. These sliders come together quickly if you use the batch-cooking Persian Beef Kabobs (see p. 13). The bean mixture can be made ahead and stored in the fridge for 3 to 5 days. It can be eaten warm or cold.

Canned refried beans (see Tip, below)	1/3 cup	75 mL
Salsa	2 tbsp.	30 mL

Persian Beef Kabobs (see p. 13),
Small slices of Monterey Jack cheese
Small cocktail buns, halved
Shredded romaine lettuce

Combine refried beans and salsa in a small bowl. Cover and refrigerate until needed. Makes enough for 6 sliders.

Packing the lunch kit: Cut kabob in half lengthwise and place both halves side by side. Warm in microwave until kabob is heated through. Cover with 1 slice of cheese and microwave until cheese is melted. Transfer to a warmed insulated container.

If you want bean mixture to be warm, reheat a portion in microwave and pack in a warmed insulated container. For a cold bean mixture, pack a portion in a container and place in an insulated lunch bag alongside lettuce container with a cooler pack to keep everything cool. Place bun in a separate container. Makes 1 slider.

At lunchtime place kabob on bottom half of bun and top with bean mixture and lettuce. Top with other half of bun and enjoy.

Tip: If you don't use the full can of refried beans, you can keep the remainder for a day or two in the fridge. The beans also freeze well, so portion them in 1/4- to 1/3-cup (60 to 75 mL) amounts and freeze for later use.

DIY Pizza

Kids will love this homemade version of the popular commercially prepared make-your-own pizza kits; not only is this version tasty and fun, but your kids can customize their pizzas by choosing their favourite ingredients. If your kids are not fond of cold pita rounds, use round wheat crackers instead. Add a selection of fresh fruit and toss in a small brownie or cookie as a special treat. Don't forget to pack a spoon for spreading the pizza sauce.

Mini pita pockets	2	2
Pizza sauce	1 tbsp.	15 mL
Pepperoni slices	8	8
Grated Mozzarella cheese	1/4 cup	60 mL
Grated medium Cheddar cheese	1/4 cup	60 mL

Packing the lunch kit: Pack each ingredient in a separate reusable container and place in an insulated lunch bag with a cooler pack to keep everything cool. Makes 1 serving.

At lunchtime, spread pitas with pizza sauce and sprinkle with toppings.

Mini Meatball Subs

Heat the meatballs and sauce in the morning as you eat breakfast, or if you are really pressed for time, prepare it the night before and pop it in the microwave in the morning to reheat. Packing the buns, cheese and basil in separate reusable containers helps keep everything fresh until lunchtime. This recipe is for 2 subs, so adjust quantities according to how many people you need to feed.

Tomato or pasta sauce	1/2 cup	125 mL
Meatballs (see p. 14)	6	6
Small oval sub buns	2	2
Grated Mozzarella cheese	1/4 cup	60 mL
Torn basil leaves (optional)	2 tbsp.	30 mL

Heat tomato sauce in a small saucepan over medium. Add meatballs and heat, stirring occasionally, until heated through.

Packing the lunch kit: Transfer meatballs to a warmed insulated container. Pack cheese and basil in separate containers and place in an insulated lunch bag with a cooler pack to keep them cool. Pack buns in a separate container.

At lunchtime, open sub buns and spoon 3 meatballs and sauce onto each bun. Sprinkle with cheese and basil, if using. Makes 2 mini subs.

Chicken Fajitas

The fajita mix can be made ahead and stored in the fridge for 3 to 4 days. For a quick shortcut, use a batch of cooked Seasoned Chicken Strips (see p. 16) in place of the chicken in this recipe. Warm it in the pan as you are cooking the peppers and onion. We've kept the fajitas simple, topping them only with sour cream and salsa, but feel free to add other fajita faves such as shredded lettuce, grated Cheddar or Monterey Jack cheese, guacamole and even kernel corn.

Canola oil	2 tsp.	10 mL
Boneless, skinless chicken breast, cut into strips	1 1/2 lbs.	680 g
Salt	1/8 tsp.	0.5 mL
Chopped onion	1 cup	250 mL
Red pepper strips	1 cup	250 mL
Yellow pepper strips	1 cup	250 mL
Chili powder	1 tbsp.	15 mL
Ground cumin	2 tsp.	10 mL
Garlic powder	1/2 tsp.	2 mL
Cayenne pepper (optional)	1/4 tsp.	1 mL
All-purpose flour	2 tbsp.	30 mL
Prepared chicken broth	1 cup	250 mL

Flour tortillas (9 inch, 23 cm, in diameter)
Sour cream
Salsa

Heat canola oil in a large frying pan on medium-high. Add chicken and sprinkle with salt. Cook, stirring often, until chicken is golden and cooked through, about 5 minutes.

Add next 7 ingredients. Cook for about 5 to 8 minutes, stirring often, until onion is softened.

Sprinkle with flour. Heat, stirring, for 1 minute. Slowly add broth, stirring constantly until boiling and thickened. Makes 6 cups (1.5 L).

Packing the lunch kit: Reheat a portion of the chicken mixture in the microwave and transfer to a warmed insulated container. Pack sour cream and salsa in separate leakproof containers and place in an insulated lunch bag with a cooler pack to keep cool. Gently fold tortilla in half and pack in a container.

At lunchtime, spread chicken mixture on tortilla and dab sour cream and salsa over top. Roll tortilla up to enclose filling.

Falafel Pita Pockets

These falafel pitas are quite substantial, so one is more than enough for smaller appetites. You can use falafel patties or balls in this recipe; patties will stay in the pita better, but balls are more fun. Don't forget to pack a spoon for spreading the sauce.

Tahini (sesame paste)	1/4 cup	60 mL
Lemon juice	2 tbsp.	30 mL
Dried oregano	1/2 tsp.	2 mL
Salt	1/4 tsp.	1 mL
Water	2 tbsp.	30 mL
Falafel patties or balls (see p. 17)	6	6
Pita pockets, split	1	1
Lettuce leaves	1 cup	250 mL
Large tomato slices, halved	2	2
Cucumber slices, thinly sliced	6	6

For the sauce, combine first 5 ingredients in a small bowl, stirring until smooth. Makes about 1/2 cup (125 mL) sauce.

Packing the lunch kit: Warm falafels in microwave until heated through and transfer to a warmed insulated container to keep warm. Pack lettuce, tomato, cucumber and a portion of sauce in separate containers and place in an insulated lunch bag with a cooler pack to keep cool. Pack pitas in an airtight container or resealable plastic bag.

At lunchtime, open pita pocket and spread sauce inside. Place lettuce, tomato and cucumber in pita and top with falafels. Press together gently. Makes 2 pita pockets.

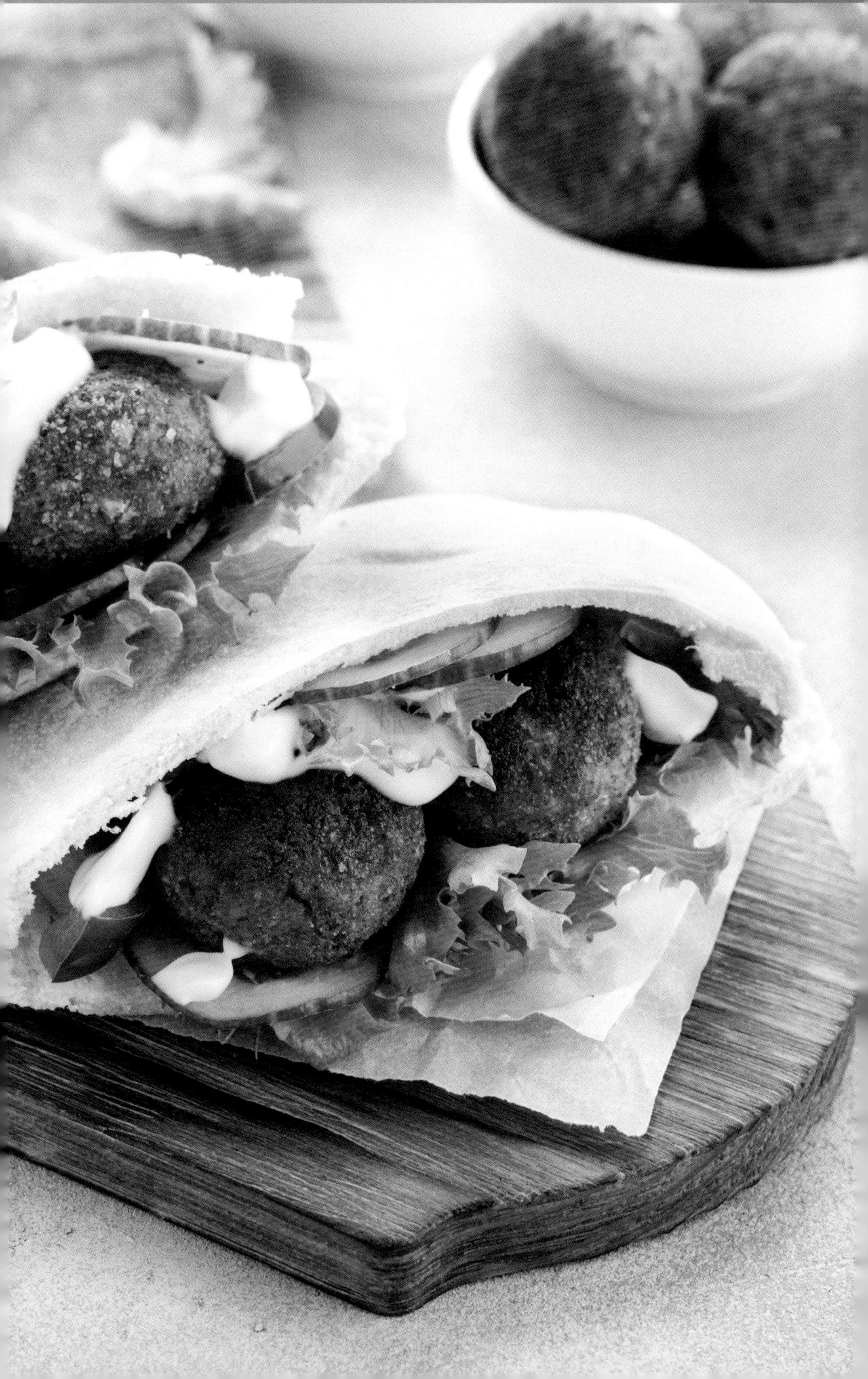

Apple Pancake Sandwich

For this sandwich you can make the pancakes in advance and then either warm them up and pack them in an insulated container or serve them cold. The sandwich is delicious either way. Be sure not to overcook the apple mixture. You do not want your apples to be mushy. The pancakes freeze beautifully, and the apple mixture can be stored in the fridge for about 3 days, but we don't recommend freezing it.

Butter	1/4 cup	60 mL
Cooking apples (such as McIntosh or Granny Smith), cored and thinly sliced	6	6
Brown sugar	1/2 cup	125 mL
Cinnamon	1 tsp.	5 mL
Lemon juice	2 tsp.	10 mL
All-purpose flour	3/4 cup	175 mL
Whole-wheat flour	3/4 cup	175 mL
Brown sugar, packed	2 tbsp.	30 mL
Baking powder	1 tbsp.	15 mL
Baking soda	1/2 tsp.	2 mL
Salt	1/4 tsp.	1 mL
Egg yolks (large)	2	2
Buttermilk (or soured milk, see Tip, p. 24)	1 1/2 cups	375 mL
Cooking oil	3 tbsp.	45 mL
Egg whites (large)	2	2

For the apples, melt butter over medium heat in a large frying pan. Add next 4 ingredients and stir to combine. Cook, stirring frequently, until apples begin to soften, about 5 minutes. Do not overcook. Set aside.

For the pancakes, combine next 6 ingredients in a medium bowl. Make a well in centre.

Whisk next 3 ingredients in a small bowl. Add to well and stir until just moistened. Batter will be lumpy.

Beat egg whites in a separate small bowl until stiff peaks form. Fold into batter. Heat a medium frying pan on medium. Spray with cooking spray and pour batter into pan, using about 1/3 cup (75 mL) for each pancake. Cook for about 3 minutes until bubbles form on top and edges appear dry. Turn pancakes over. Cook for about 3 minutes until golden. Remove to a large plate. Repeat with remaining batter, spraying frying pan with cooking spray if necessary to prevent sticking. Makes about 12 pancakes.

Packing the lunch kit: Reheat apple mixture in the microwave until warmed through. Transfer to a warmed insulated container. Place pancakes in a separate container.

At lunchtime, spoon apple mixture onto 1 pancake and top with a second pancake.

Spicy Tortilla Chips with Chili

These homemade tortilla chips are only mildly spicy. If your kids like a little heat, feel free to up the amount of cayenne pepper you use. The chips will stay crisp for about 5 days when stored in an airtight container.

Butter (or hard margarine), softened	3/4 cup	175 mL
Grated Parmesan cheese	1/2 cup	125 mL
Sesame seeds	1/4 cup	60 mL
Parsley flakes	2 tsp.	10 mL
Dried whole oregano	1/2 tsp.	2 mL
Onion powder	1/4 tsp.	1 mL
Garlic powder	1/4 tsp.	1 mL
Cayenne pepper	1/4 tsp.	1 mL
Flour tortillas (6 inch, 15 cm, diameter)	12	12

Chili (see p. 12)

For the tortilla chips, combine first 8 ingredients in a small bowl.

Spread a thick layer of Parmesan cheese mixture on each tortilla. It will seem like too much but once cooked they will be just right. Cut each tortilla into 8 wedges. Arrange in a single layer on ungreased baking sheets. Bake in 350°F (175°C) oven for 12 to 15 minutes until crisp and golden. Makes 96 crisps.

Packing the lunch kit: Reheat chili in the microwave and transfer to a warmed insulated container. Package a portion of tortilla chips in a separate container.

Meatballs with Tzatziki

Make the tzatziki in advance and use the batch-cooking Meatballs (see p. 14) to make this lunch quick and easy to prepare. The tzatziki will last for about 3 days in the fridge but does not freeze. Make sure the container you choose for the tzatziki is leakproof and wide enough for dipping the meatballs. To up the fun factor, pack toothpicks instead of a fork for dipping the meatballs. Make sure you trim the sharp ends off the toothpicks if your kids will be tempted to use them as swords with their classmates.

Balkan-style plain yogurt, well drained (see Tip, below)	1 cup	250 mL
Large seedless cucumber, peeled and grated	1/2	1/2
Chopped fresh dill	3 tbsp.	45 mL
Lemon juice	2 tbsp.	30 mL
Garlic cloves, minced	3	3
Salt, to taste		
Pepper, to taste		

Meatballs (see p. 14)

For the tzatziki, combine yogurt, cucumber, dill, lemon juice, garlic, salt and pepper in a medium bowl. Stir until well combined. Let stand, covered, in refrigerator for at least 1 hour to allow flavours to blend. Makes 1 1/2 cups (375 mL).

Packing the lunch kit: Reheat meatballs in the microwave or heat them in 375°F (190°C) oven for about 10 minutes until warmed through. Transfer to a warmed insulated container to keep warm. Fill a small leakproof container with tzatziki and place in an insulated lunch bag with a cooler pack to keep tzatziki cool.

Tip: To drain the yogurt, place a fine-mesh strainer over a bowl and line it with cheesecloth or a coffee filter. Pour the yogurt into the strainer and let stand in the refrigerator for at least two hours.

Pizza Sticks

We stuck to the basic pepperoni and cheese pizza in this recipe, but feel free to add whatever toppings you prefer. The pizza can be made up to 2 days in advance, but we suggest that you don't cut it into sticks until after you've reheated it. We've paired the pizza sticks with ranch dressing, but use whatever dip your child likes to dunk their pizza in. Warm marinara sauce would also work well.

Prepared pizza sauce	3 tbsp.	45 mL
Naan bread	1	1
Pepperoni slices	12	12
Grated Mozzarella cheese	1/2 cup	125 mL
Chopped fresh basil (optional)	2 tbsp.	30 mL
Ranch dressing	1/4 cup	60 mL

Spread pizza sauce on naan bread and top with pepperoni slices. Sprinkle with cheese. Transfer to a baking sheet and cook in 375°F (190°C) oven for 12 minutes until cheese is bubbly.

Sprinkle with basil. Makes 1 serving.

Packing the lunch kit: Reheat pizza in a toaster oven until warmed through. Set aside to cool slightly and then cut into 6 slices. Transfer to a warmed insulated container to keep warm. Fill a small leakproof container with ranch dressing and place in an insulated lunch bag with a cooler pack to keep dressing cool.

Chicken Nuggets

These chicken nuggets have a texture that is similar to those offered by a favourite fast food franchise, but they are much healthier. They can be made ahead and stored in the fridge for up to 3 days or frozen for up to 3 months. For best results reheat in a toaster oven or oven. We've paired the nuggets with barbecue sauce, but sweet-and-sour or honey mustard sauce would also be good options.

Ground chicken	1 lb.	454 g
Mashed potatoes	3/4 cups	175 mL
Chopped fresh parsley	2 tbsp.	30 mL
Garlic powder	1/2 tsp.	2 mL
Onion powder	1/2 tsp.	2 mL
Salt	1/2 tsp.	2 mL
Pepper	1/4 tsp.	1 mL
Flour	3/4 cup	175 mL
Garlic powder	1/2 tsp.	2 mL
Onion powder	1/2 tsp.	2 mL
Salt	1/4 tsp.	1 mL
Large eggs	2	2
Water	1/4 cup	60 mL
Dried bread crumbs	1 cup	250 mL
Dried parsley	1 tsp.	5 mL
Poultry seasoning	1/2 tsp.	2 mL
Prepared barbecue sauce		

Combine first 7 ingredients in a large bowl. Shape chicken mixture into nugget-like shapes using 1 1/2 tbsp. (22 mL) for each.

Combine next 4 ingredients on a shallow dish.

Beat eggs and water together in a separate bowl.

Combine next 3 ingredients in a separate dish. Toss chicken nuggets in flour mixture. Gently coat in egg mixture allowing excess to drip off, and then coat in bread crumb mixture. Place each piece on a prepared baking sheet. Bake in 400°F (200°C) oven for 40 minutes, flipping nuggets over halfway through cooking time. Makes about 20 nuggets.

Packing the lunch kit: Reheat nuggets in a toaster oven or oven until warmed through. Transfer to a warmed insulated container. Transfer a portion of barbecue sauce to a leakproof container.

Baked Spring Rolls with Plum Sauce

These spring rolls have all the flavour of the deep-fried version but without all the added fat and are delicious with our simple homemade plum sauce. The rolls will keep in the fridge for up to 3 days. For best results, reheat in a toaster oven or oven. The plum sauce will keep for about 5 days in the fridge and can also be frozen.

Plum jam	1 cup	250 mL
Cider vinegar	3 tbsp.	45 mL
Granulated sugar	2 tsp.	10 mL
Canola oil	2 tsp.	10 mL
Lean ground pork	1/2 lb.	225 g
Canola oil	1 tsp.	5 mL
Finely chopped onion	1 cup	250 mL
Thinly sliced carrot	1 cup	250 mL
Shredded Napa cabbage (optional)	1/4 cup	60 mL
Thinly sliced bamboo shoots	1 cup	250 mL
Soy sauce	2 tbsp.	30 mL
Finely grated gingerroot (or 3/4 tsp., 4 mL, ground ginger)	1 tbsp.	15 mL
Garlic cloves, minced	2	2
Chili paste (sambal oelek), optional	1/2 tsp.	2 mL
Hoisin sauce	1 tsp.	5 mL
Phyllo pastry sheets, thawed according to package directions	16	16

For the plum sauce, combine first 3 ingredients in a medium bowl. If mixture contains many skins, strain it through a fine-mesh sieve. Makes about 1 cup (250 mL).

For the spring rolls, heat first amount of canola oil in a large frying pan on medium-high. Add pork and scramble-fry for about 5 minutes until no longer pink. Drain and transfer to a medium bowl. Set aside.

Heat second amount of canola oil in same frying pan on medium. Add onion, carrot and cabbage and cook for about 5 minutes, stirring often, until onion starts to soften.

Add next 6 ingredients and cook, stirring, for about 5 minutes until liquid is evaporated. Add to pork and stir gently.

Place 1 pastry sheet on a work surface with longest side closest to you. Cover remaining sheets with a damp towel to prevent drying. Spray sheet with cooking spray. Place second sheet on top. Spray with cooking spray. Fold in half crosswise. Spray with cooking spray. Place about 1/2 cup (125 mL) pork mixture across bottom of sheet, leaving 1 inch (2.5 cm) border on each side. Fold sides over filling. Roll up from bottom to enclose filling. Brush edge with water to seal. Place, seam-side down, on a greased baking sheet with sides. Cover rolls with separate damp towel to prevent drying. Repeat with remaining pastry sheets and pork mixture. Spray rolls with cooking spray. Bake in 375°F (190°C) oven for about 25 minutes until browned. Makes 8 spring rolls.

Packing the lunch kit: Reheat spring rolls in a toaster oven or oven until warmed through. Transfer to a warmed insulated container. Transfer a portion of plum sauce to a leakproof container.

Asian Chicken Salad Rolls

We've paired these salad rolls with a sweet chili sauce but they would also be delicious with a peanut sauce, if your school is nut friendly. Make the salad rolls up to 2 days in advance, wrap them individually in plastic wrap and store in an airtight container in the fridge. Do not freeze. You could use the batch-cooking Seasoned Chicken Strips (see p. 16) for the cooked chicken, if you have any on hand.

Rice vermicelli, broken up	2 1/2 oz.	70 g
Finely chopped cooked chicken (see p. 16)	3/4 cup	175 mL
Chopped romaine lettuce, lightly packed	1/2 cup	125 mL
Grated carrot	1/3 cup	75 mL
Medium cucumber, peeled and thinly sliced	1/2	1/2
Chopped fresh cilantro (or parsley)	2 tbsp.	30 mL
Sesame oil (for flavour)	1 tsp.	5 mL
Salt	1/8 tsp.	0.5 mL
Rice paper rounds (6 inch, 15 cm, diameter)	16	16

Sweet chili sauce

Place vermicelli in a small heatproof bowl. Cover with boiling water and let stand for about 5 minutes until tender. Drain and rinse with cold water. Drain well. Transfer to a medium bowl.

Add next 7 ingredients and toss gently.

Place 1 rice paper round in a shallow bowl of hot water until just softened. Place on a work surface. Spoon about 1/4 cup (60 mL) chicken mixture across centre. Fold sides over filling. Roll up tightly from bottom to enclose filling. Transfer to a plate and cover with a damp towel to prevent drying. Repeat with remaining rice paper rounds and chicken mixture. Makes 16 rolls.

Packing the lunch kit: Pack individually wrapped salad roll in an insulated lunch bag with a cooler pack. Transfer a portion of sweet chili sauce to a leakproof container and place in lunch bag.

Falafel with Curry Yogurt Dip

Falafel balls (or patties) dipped in a creamy curry yogurt dip—these are sure to be the envy of the classroom! Depending on your child's appetite, 5 or 6 falafel balls would be a good serving size. For best results reheat the falafel in the oven or toaster oven. The dip can be made ahead and refrigerated for 3 to 5 days.

Plain yogurt	1/2 cup	125 mL
Mayonnaise	1 tbsp.	15 mL
Curry powder	1 tsp.	5 mL
Liquid honey	1/2 tsp.	2 mL
Salt, to taste		
Pepper, to taste		

Falafel balls or patties (see p. 17)

For the dip, combine first 6 ingredients in a small bowl. Chill, covered, for at least 30 minutes to blend flavours. Makes about 1/2 cup (125 mL).

Packing the lunch kit: Reheat falafel on an ungreased baking sheet in a 400°F (200°C) toaster oven or oven until crisp and warmed through. Transfer to a warmed insulated container. Transfer a portion of curry yogurt dip to a leakproof container and place in an insulated lunch bag with a cooler pack.

Sweet Potato Ravioli

Ready-to-use wonton wrappers replace the traditional pasta sheets in these cheesy ravioli, which are stuffed with a savoury sweet potato filling. Make the ravioli in advance and store in the fridge for 3 to 5 days. To freeze, spread the ravioli out in a single layer on a baking sheet and place in the freezer until firm, then transfer the frozen ravioli to a container or freezer bag. Pair with your favourite homemade or prepared marina sauce for dipping, and don't forget to pack a fork as the marinara sauce will be warm.

Chopped peeled orange-fleshed sweet potato	4 cups	1 L
Goat (chèvre) cheese, cut up	3 oz.	85 g
Smoked (sweet) paprika	1 tsp.	5 mL
Salt	1/2 tsp.	2 mL
Pepper	1/2 tsp.	2 mL
Wonton wrappers (see Tip, below)	72	72
Butter (or hard margarine)		
Marinara sauce		

Pour water into a large saucepan until about 1 inch (2.5 cm) deep. Add sweet potato and bring to a boil. Reduce heat to medium and boil gently, covered, for 12 to 15 minutes until sweet potato is tender. Drain and mash.

Add next 4 ingredients. Mash until combined.

Arrange 36 wrappers on a work surface. Place 1 tbsp. (15 mL) sweet potato mixture in centre of each wrapper. Brush water over edges of wrappers. Cover with remaining wrappers and press edges to seal.

Cook half of ravioli in boiling, salted water for about 5 minutes, stirring occasionally, until wrappers are tender but firm. Transfer with a slotted spoon to a strainer. Drain well. Repeat with remaining ravioli. Makes 6 servings.

Packing the lunch kit: Heat butter in a frying pan on medium, using about 1/2 tbsp. (7 mL) butter per portion of ravioli. Cook for about 2 minutes per side. Transfer to a warmed insulated container. Microwave a portion of marinara sauce until piping hot and transfer to a warmed insulated container.

Tip: Look for wonton wrappers in the produce section of grocery stores with other fresh noodles or in the Asian section of the freezer department.

Sweet Potato Nuggets with Chipotle Lime Dip

Kids love potato nuggets or "tots," but commercially prepared versions are deep fried and loaded with salt. We've given the traditional potato nuggets a healthy, tasty makeover by using sweet potato instead of regular potato and baking them in the oven. The end result is slightly sweet and perfectly crunchy, just like a potato nugget should be! To store, arrange the nuggets in a single layer on a baking sheet and freeze until firm. Transfer to a freezer bag or container and store in the freezer for up to 3 months. The dip will last in an airtight container in the fridge for 3 to 5 days.

Medium sweet potatoes, peeled and cut into even pieces	2	2
All-purpose flour	2 tbsp.	30 mL
Garlic clove, minced	1	1
Salt	1 tsp.	5 mL
Chili powder	1/2 tsp.	2 mL
Panko bread crumbs	1 1/2 cups	375 mL
Chopped fresh parsley	3 tbsp.	45 mL
Light sour cream	1/2 cup	125 mL
Light mayonnaise	1/2 cup	125 mL
Lime juice	1/4 cup	60 mL
Chopped fresh cilantro or parsley	1/4 cup	60 mL
Minced chipotle peppers in adobo sauce	1 tsp.	5 mL
Grated lime zest (see Tip, p. 126)	2 tsp.	10 mL

Cook sweet potato in boiling water in a large pot or Dutch oven on medium-high until soft but not mushy. Drain and mash. Use cheesecloth or a clean tea towel to squeeze excess water out of sweet potato.

Stir in next 4 ingredients. When mixture is cool enough to handle, scoop out 1 tbsp. (15 mL) and roll into a nugget shape. Repeat with remaining mixture.

Combine panko and parsley in a shallow bowl. Roll sweet potato nuggets in crumb mixture until evenly coated. Transfer to a greased baking sheet and bake in 400°F (200°C) oven for 30 minutes, flipping nuggets halfway through. Makes about 42 nuggets.

For the dip, combine remaining 6 ingredients in a small bowl. Makes about 1 1/3 cups (325 mL).

Packing the lunch kit: Reheat nuggets in a 400°F (200°C) oven or toaster oven until warmed through. Transfer to a warmed insulated container. Transfer a portion of dip to a leakproof container and place in an insulated lunch bag with a cooler pack.

Avocado Hummus with Pita

Love guacamole and hummus? Well, with this avocado hummus, you get the best of both worlds! It can be stored be stored in an airtight container for up to 4 days, but the colour will fade the longer it sits. Do not freeze.

Can of chickpeas (19 oz., 540 mL) rinsed and drained	1	1
Large avocado, seeded, peeled and coarsely chopped	1	1
Olive (or cooking) oil	1/4 cup	60 mL
Lemon juice	2 tbsp.	30 mL
Roasted sesame seeds	2 tbsp.	30 mL
Chopped fresh parsley (or 3/4 tsp., 4 mL, flakes)	1 tbsp.	15 mL
Garlic cloves, chopped (or 1/2 tsp., 2 mL, powder)	2	2
Salt	1/2 tsp.	2 mL
Pepper	1/4 tsp.	1 mL

Pita bread, cut into triangles

For the hummus, process first 8 ingredients in a food processor until smooth. Makes about 1 3/4 cups (425 mL).

Packing the lunch kit: Transfer a portion of hummus to a leakproof container and place in an insulated lunch bag with a cooler pack. Place pita triangles in an airtight container.

Veggie "Chips" and Guacamole

If your kids love chips and dip, this might just be the perfect lunch for them. The tasty guacamole pairs perfectly with sliced veggies for a healthy, satisfying meal that feels like a special treat.

Mashed avocado	1 1/2 cups	375 mL
Chopped seeded tomato	1/2 cup	125 mL
Finely chopped yellow pepper	1/4 cup	60 mL
Thinly sliced green onion	3 tbsp.	45 mL
Lime juice	2 tbsp.	30 mL
Chopped fresh cilantro (or parsley)	1 tbsp.	15 mL
Cooking oil	2 tsp.	10 mL
Garlic clove, minced	1	1
(or 1/4 tsp., 1 mL, powder)		
Salt	1/2 tsp.	2 mL
Pepper	1/4 tsp.	1 mL

Peeled jicama sticks
Orange pepper slices
Diagonally sliced zucchini coins

For the guacamole, combine first 10 ingredients in a medium bowl. Makes about 2 1/2 cups (625 mL).

Packing the lunch kit: Transfer a portion of guacamole to a leakproof container and place in an insulated lunch bag with a cooler pack. Add a selection of jicama, orange pepper and zucchini to a container and place in lunch bag with guacamole.

Fruit Skewers with Blueberry Dip

You can use your favourite combination of fruit for the skewers; just remember to trim the sharp tip of the skewer with scissors once the fruit is on to prevent any swordplay at school. Store any leftover dip in the fridge in an airtight container for 3 to 5 days, or pour it into ice pop moulds and freeze for 3 to 4 hours until firm for a frosty after-school snack.

Frozen mixed berries, thawed	1 cup	250 mL
Spreadable cream cheese	1/2 cup	125 mL
Vanilla yogurt	1/2 cup	125 mL
Berry jam	1/4 cup	60 mL

Bamboo skewers (8 inch, 20 cm, each)
Strawberries
Pineapple chunks
Honeydew balls
Cantaloupe balls
Watermelon chunks
Blackberries
Kiwi slices
Orange slices

For the dip, combine first 4 ingredients in a blender until smooth. Makes about 1 1/2 cups (375 mL).

Packing the lunch kit: Thread your choice of fruit onto skewers and trim the sharp tip with scissors. Transfer to an insulated lunch bag. Fill a chilled insulated container with dip, or use a small leakproof container and place it in insulated lunch bag alongside skewers, adding a cooler pack to keep everything cool.

French Toast Sticks with Maple Yogurt Dip

Who doesn't love breakfast for lunch? Or supper? Kids will love dunking the French toast sticks into the creamy yogurt dip. Use the batch-cooking French Toast recipe (see p. 20) and make the dip ahead. It will store in the fridge for 4 to 5 days but does not freeze well.

Thick vanilla yogurt (see Tip, below)	1 cup	250 mL
Maple syrup	3 tbsp.	45 mL
Cinnamon	2 tsp.	10 mL

French toast slices (see p. 20)

For the dip, combine first 3 ingredients in a small bowl, stirring until well combined. Makes 2 servings.

Packing the lunch kit: Use a toaster to reheat French toast slices or bake them in 375°F (190°C) oven for 5 to 10 minutes. Cut each toast into 4 pieces lengthwise and place in an insulated container to keep warm. Fill a small leakproof container with dip and place it in an insulated lunch bag with a cooler pack to keep the dip cool.

Tip: Greek, skyr (Icelandic) or Balkan-style yogurt would all work well in this recipe.

Charoset with Waffle Sticks

Traditionally eaten at Passover, charoset is simple to make and oh so delicious. If your school has a no-nut policy, you could try substituting pumpkin or sunflower seeds, but the flavour will not be the same. We've paired it with waffles (see p. 21) but you could also use crackers or pita chips. Store the charoset for up to 3 days in an airtight container in the fridge. Do not freeze.

Granny Smith apples, cored and cut into chunks	2	2
Gala apple, cored and cut into chunks	1	1
Chopped walnuts	2/3 cup	150 mL
Ground cinnamon	2 tsp.	10 mL
Lemon juice	2 tbsp.	30 mL
Liquid honey	3 tbsp.	45 mL
Brown sugar, to taste (optional)		
Waffles (see p. 21)		

For the charoset, combine first 5 ingredients in a food processor and pulse until well combined. Transfer to a medium bowl.

Stir in honey until well combined. Sprinkle individual servings with brown sugar, if desired. Makes 6 servings.

Packing the lunch kit: Use a toaster to reheat waffles and cut each waffle into sticks. Transfer to a warmed insulated container to keep warm. Place a portion of charoset in a small leakproof container and place in an insulated lunch bag with a cooler pack.

Mini Shepherd's Pies

These cute little shepherd's pies are the perfect size for little hands. They will keep in the fridge for 4 to 5 days and can be frozen for up to 3 months. Cool completely before freezing, and reheat from frozen. To reheat, you can pop them in the microwave or place them in a 375°F (190°C) oven until warmed through.

Medium sweet potatoes, peeled and cut into large chunks	4	4
Milk	2 tbsp.	30 mL
Butter	1 tbsp.	15 mL
Salt	1/4 tsp.	1 mL
Cooking oil	1/2 tsp.	2 mL
Lean ground beef	3/4 lb.	340 g
Chopped onion	1/4 cup	60 mL
All-purpose flour	1/2 tbsp.	7 mL
Salt	1 tsp.	5 mL
Pepper	1/8 tsp.	0.5 mL
Milk	1/4 cup	60 mL
Frozen peas, thawed	1/2 cup	125 mL
Chopped carrots	1/2 cup	125 mL
Kernel corn	1/2 cup	125 mL
Tomato paste	1 tbsp.	15 mL
Pastry for 2 crust (9 inch, 25 cm) pie shell		
Butter, melted	2 tbsp.	30 mL

In a medium saucepan, cook sweet potatoes in boiling salted water until tender. Drain. Add next 3 ingredients and mash, making sure mixture is well combined. Cover and set aside.

Heat cooking oil in a large frying pan on medium. Add beef and onion and scramble fry until beef is no longer pink inside, about 6 to 8 minutes. Drain.

Stir in next 3 ingredients. Slowly stir in second amount of milk. Heat, stirring constantly, for about 2 minutes, until thickened. Stir in next 4 ingredients and remove from heat.

Roll pie dough out on a lightly floured surface into a 9 x 12 inch (23 x 30 cm) rectangle. Cut into 12 even squares. Place 1 square into each cup of a greased muffin pan and press gently into bottom and up sides of cup. Fill each cup evenly with ground beef mixture. Spread or pipe sweet potato mixture evenly over top of ground beef mixture and brush with melted butter. Bake in 375°F (190°C) oven for 18 to 20 minutes, until sweet potatoes are browned. Transfer to a wire rack to cool before removing from pan. Makes 12 mini shepherd's pies.

Packing the lunch kit: Reheat shepherd's pie in a microwave or 375°F (190°C) oven until warmed through (about 10 minutes if not frozen, and 15 to 20 minutes if frozen). Transfer to a warmed insulated container.

Mac and Cheese Cups

A perennial childhood favourite in a convenient hand-held form! These cheesy cups can be made ahead and stored in the fridge for 3 to 5 days or frozen for about 2 months. For best results, reheat in the oven or toaster oven instead of the microwave. Use sharp Cheddar for a stronger flavour.

Bacon slices, chopped	6	6
Elbow macaroni	3 cups	750 mL
Butter	1/4 cup	60 mL
All-purpose flour	1/3 cup	75 mL
Milk, warmed	3 cups	750 mL
Salt	1/2 tsp.	2 mL
Ground nutmeg	1/2 tsp.	2 mL
Dry mustard	1/4 tsp.	1 mL
Pepper	1/8 tsp.	0.5 mL
Grated medium Cheddar cheese	3 cups	750 mL
Butter	3 tbsp.	45 mL
Panko bread crumbs	1/2 cup	125 mL
Grated medium Cheddar cheese	1/4 cup	60 mL

Cook bacon in a medium pan on medium until crisp, about 6 minutes. Remove with a slotted spoon to a plate lined with paper towel to drain. Set aside.

Cook macaroni according to package directions until tender but firm. Drain and set aside.

Melt first amount of butter in same saucepan on medium-low heat. Add flour and heat, stirring, for 1 minute. Slowly add milk, whisking constantly, until smooth. Heat, stirring, for about 5 minutes until simmering and thickened.

Add next 4 ingredients and cook, stirring, for 1 minute. Remove from heat. Add first amount of cheese, stirring until melted. Stir in macaroni and bacon. Set aside.

Heat second amount of butter in a small saucepan on medium. Remove from heat and stir in panko and second amount of cheese. Scoop macaroni mixture into greased muffin cups and sprinkle each muffin cup evenly with panko mixture. Bake in 375°F (190°C) oven for 15 to 20 minutes until golden brown. Place pan on a wire rack to cool. Allow mac and cheese cups to cool well before removing from pan. Makes 12 cups.

Packing the lunch kit: Reheat cups in a toaster oven or oven until warmed through. Transfer to a warmed insulated container.

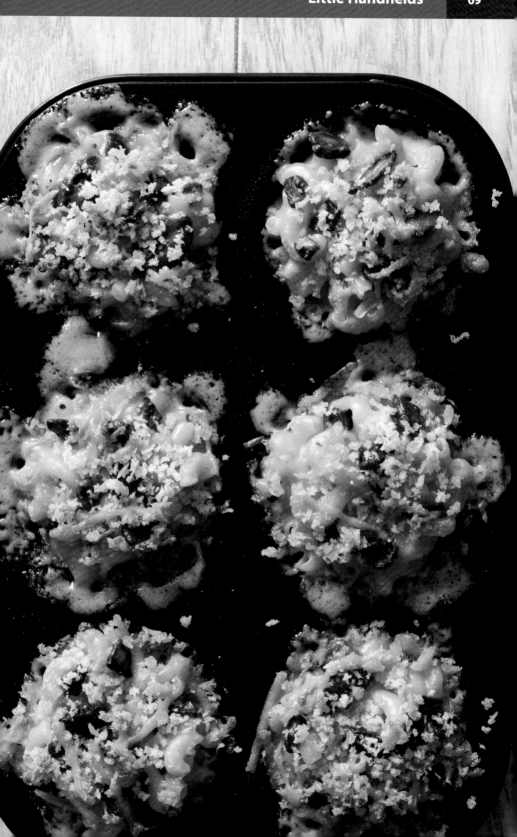

Omelette Cups

As a short cut, use the batch-cooking Breakfast Sausage (see p. 15) in place of the uncooked breakfast sausage. Simply crumble it and add it to the onions as they are cooking. The omelette cups can be made ahead and stored in an airtight container in the fridge for up to 5 days or frozen for about 3 months. They can be served warm or cold.

Cooking oil	1 tbsp.	15 mL
Breakfast sausage, crumbled	3/4 lb.	340 g
Cooking oil	2 tsp.	10 mL
Finely chopped red onion	1/2 cup	125 mL
Frozen peas	1 cup	250 mL
Grated fresh Parmesan cheese	2/3 cup	150 mL
Chopped fresh mint	2 tbsp.	30 mL
(or 1 1/2 tsp., 7 mL, dried)		
Large eggs	8	8
Milk	1/2 cup	125 mL
Salt	1/4 tsp.	1 mL
Pepper	1/4 tsp.	1 mL

Heat first amount of cooking oil in a large frying pan on medium. Add sausage and cook, stirring, until no longer pink. Transfer to a medium bowl.

Heat second amount of cooking oil in same frying pan on medium. Add onion and cook for about 5 minutes, stirring often, until softened. Add to sausage.

Add next 3 ingredients to sausage mixture and stir until well combined. Spoon sausage mixture into 12 well-greased muffin cups.

Whisk remaining 4 ingredients in a medium bowl until smooth. Pour over sausage mixture in muffin cups. Bake in 350°F (175°C) oven for about 30 minutes until golden and set. Let stand in pan for 5 minutes. Run knife around omelette cups to loosen. Remove to a wire rack to cool. Makes 12 omelette cups.

Packing the lunch kit: If serving cold, transfer cups to an insulated lunch bag and add a cooler pack. If serving warm, reheat cups in microwave until heated through and transfer to a warmed insulated container.

Out-the-door Rolls

These rolls taste best warm, but they are also scrumptious cold. The dough must be chilled for at least 30 minutes before cooking, so to save time in the morning, prepare the rolls the evening before, leave them in the fridge overnight, and pop them in the oven when you get up so they can cook as you are getting ready for your day. You can also prepare the dish in its entirety in advance if your mornings are particularly rushed, then reheat the rolls in the oven or toaster oven until warmed through. The rolls will keep for up to 5 days in the fridge and up to 3 months in the freezer.

All-purpose flour	2 1/4 cups	300 mL
Granulated sugar	1 tbsp.	15 mL
Baking powder	2 tsp.	10 mL
Salt	1/2 tsp.	2 mL
Cooking oil	1/4 cup	60 mL
Milk	3/4 cup	175 mL
Lean ground pork	1 lb.	454 g
Lemon juice	1 1/2 tbsp.	25 mL
Diced green pepper	1/2 cup	125 mL
Diced red pepper	1/2 cup	125 mL
Chili powder	2 tsp.	10 mL
Dried oregano	3/4 tsp.	4 mL
Garlic powder	1/4 tsp.	1 mL
Paprika	1/2 tsp.	2 mL
Salt	1 tsp.	5 mL
Pepper	1/4 tsp.	1 mL

Combine flour, sugar, baking powder and salt in a large bowl. Add cooking oil and milk. Stir to form a soft ball. Knead dough 10 times on lightly floured surface. Line a 10 x 15 inch (25 x 38 cm) jelly roll pan with waxed paper to use as a guide for size. Roll dough to fit size of pan. Pat lightly with your hand to make an even layer.

Combine remaining 10 ingredients in a large bowl. Crumble mixture over dough leaving a 1/2 inch (12 mm) border all around. Use waxed paper to help roll up from longest side, removing paper as you roll. Pinch seam closed. Chill for at least 30 minutes. Cut into 1 inch (2.5 cm) slices. Arrange on greased baking sheets about 1 inch (2.5 cm) apart. Bake in 400°F (200°C) oven for 20 to 25 minutes until lightly browned. Makes 15 rolls.

Packing the lunch kit: Pack warm rolls in a warmed insulated container. If you prefer them cold, pack them in an insulated lunch bag with a cooler pack.

Ham and Egg Cups

These handy cups are super versatile. Don't like ham? Use turkey instead. Not a fan of zucchini? Try spinach or green peas. Almost any combination of meat, cheese and veggies will work, so use what your kids like best. These cups can be made ahead and stored in the fridge in an airtight container for up to 3 days or frozen for up to 1 month.

Deli ham slices, thinly sliced	12	12
Grated Cheddar cheese	1 cup	250 mL
Large egg, lightly beaten	8	8
Milk	1/4 cup	60 mL
Salt	1/4 tsp.	1 mL
Pepper	1/8 tsp.	0.5 mL
Red pepper, finely chopped	1/2 cup	125 mL
Zucchini, grated	1/2 cup	125 mL
Finely sliced green onion	2 tbsp.	30 mL

In a greased 12-cup muffin tray, line muffin cups with ham to form a ham cup. Sprinkle cheese in bottom of each ham cup.

Combine next 4 ingredients in a medium bowl.

Stir in remaining 3 ingredients. Pour mixture into prepared ham cups, ensuring ingredients are distributed evenly. Bake in 350°F (175°C) oven for 16 to 20 minutes until eggs have set. Cool for 10 minutes before removing from pan. Transfer to a wire rack to cool completely. Makes 12 ham and egg cups.

Packing the lunch kit: Reheat ham cups in microwave until warmed through and transfer to a warmed insulated container.

Bacon Roll-ups

For this recipe we've used a combination of red, orange, green and yellow peppers, but you can use any combination you like, or even all of one type, if you prefer. The roll-ups can be made in advance and stored in the fridge for up to two days. Do not freeze. They can be reheated in the microwave, or for crispier bacon, in a toaster oven or oven.

Bacon strips	6	6
Thin bell pepper slices	24	24

Wrap 1 bacon strip around 4 pepper slices, starting at the bottom of the peppers and winding your way up until only the tips of peppers are showing. Secure with a toothpick. Repeat with remaining bacon strips and pepper slices. Arrange on a baking tray with sides and bake in 400°F (200°C) oven for 10 minutes. Turn roll-ups over and bake for 10 more minutes, or until bacon has reached preferred crispiness. Remove from oven and let cool before removing toothpicks. Makes 6 roll-ups.

Packing the lunch kit: Reheat roll-ups in the microwave or oven until warmed through and transfer to a warmed insulated container.

Pizza "Sushie"

A different, fun approach to pizza with a unique presentation. We've used pepperoni and green pepper in our recipe, but you can change it up to include your child's favourite pizza toppings. The wraps need to be made in advance and rest in the refrigerator overnight so they can firm up enough to allow you to cut them into "sushie." The "sushie" can be stored in the fridge for 2 to 3 days, but they will soften the longer they sit.

Cream cheese, at room temperature	8 oz.	225 g
Pizza sauce	3/4 cup	175 mL
Italian seasoning	1 tsp.	5 mL
Flour tortillas (9 inch, 23 cm, in diameter)	5	5
Pepperoni slices, chopped	1 cup	250 mL
Chopped green pepper	3/4 cup	175 mL
Grated Mozzarella cheese	1 cup	250 mL

Combine cream cheese, pizza sauce and Italian seasoning in a medium bowl. Spread over tortillas, leaving a 1/2 inch (12 mm) border.

Combine pepperoni and green pepper in a small bowl. Sprinkle evenly over cream cheese mixture. Sprinkle cheese evenly over top. Roll tortillas up tightly and wrap in plastic wrap. Refrigerate overnight to allow sushi to firm up. Trim ends and cut each wrap into 1 inch (2.5 cm) pieces. Makes 35 pieces.

Packing the lunch kit: Place sushie pieces in an insulated container with a cooler pack.

Mini Baked Potatoes

If you send a whole baked potato with your child for lunch, it will likely come back largely uneaten. Tackling such a large portion of food can be a daunting task to a child who would just as soon be talking to friends as eating during the short lunch break. These bite-sized potatoes, however, are as enticing as they are cute. Cook the potatoes and bacon the night before and, for best results, reheat in the morning before adding the sour cream, green onion and cheese.

Unpeeled baby potatoes	18	18
Olive oil	2 tbsp.	30 mL
Bacon slices, chopped	3	3
Finely chopped green onions	3 tbsp.	45 mL
Grated Cheddar cheese	1/3 cup	75 mL
Sour cream	1/2 cup	125 mL

Prick potatoes with a fork and place in a medium bowl. Drizzle with olive oil and toss to coat. Arrange potatoes on a greased baking sheet and cook in 375°F (190°C) oven for 25 to 30 minutes. Set aside to cool. Cut a small cross in top of each potato and pinch base to open.

Cook bacon in a medium pan on medium until crisp, about 6 minutes. Remove with a slotted spoon to a plate lined with paper towel to drain. Recipe be prepared in advance to here. Makes 18 mini potatoes.

Packing the lunch kit: Reheat a portion of potatoes in the microwave and transfer to a warmed insulated container. Sprinkle with bacon bits, green onion and cheese. Pack sour cream in a leakproof container and place in an insulated lunch bag with a cooler pack.

At lunchtime, spoon a portion of sour cream over mini potatoes.

Breakfast Burritos

Why spend money on commercially prepared breakfast burritos when they are so easy to make at home? Homemade versions are healthier too, and you can customize them to include all your favourite ingredients. These burritos freeze beautifully, so make a few extra to store in the freezer for when you need a quick lunch option.

Cooking oil	2 tsp.	10 mL
Sliced onion	1 cup	250 mL
Sliced red pepper	1 cup	250 mL
Sliced yellow pepper	1 cup	250 mL
Sliced zucchini (with peel)	1 cup	250 mL
Chili powder	1 tsp.	5 mL
Ground cumin	1/2 tsp.	2 mL
Garlic clove, minced	1	1
Salt	1/4 tsp.	1 mL
Pepper	1/4 tsp.	1 mL
Cooking oil	1 tsp.	5 mL
Large eggs	6	6
Milk	1/4 cup	60 mL
Flour tortillas (9 inch, 23 cm, diameter)	6	6
Chopped avocado	1/2 cup	125 mL
Grated jalapeño Monterey Jack cheese	1/3 cup	75 mL
Cooked bacon slices, crumbled	4	4
Salsa	1/4 cup	60 mL

Heat cooking oil in a large frying pan on medium. Add next 9 ingredients. Cook for about 8 minutes, stirring often, until onion is softened. Transfer to a medium bowl and set aside. Wipe frying pan with a paper towel.

Heat second amount of cooking oil in same frying pan on medium. Whisk eggs and milk in a small bowl. Add to frying pan and reduce heat to medium-low. Stir slowly and constantly with spatula, scraping sides and bottom of pan until eggs are set and liquid is evaporated.

Arrange egg mixture along centre of each tortilla. Spoon onion mixture over egg. Top with remaining 4 ingredients. Fold sides over filling. Roll up from bottom to enclose. Makes 6 burritos.

Packing the lunch kit: Reheat burrito in the microwave until heated through and transfer to a warmed insulated container.

Beef Pasties

Pasties are a popular dish in Cornwall, and it is easy to see why. These handheld meat pies make a perfect meal on the go, and they can be eaten hot or cold. In this recipe, we have included instructions for the dough, but if you are short on time, you can use prepared pie dough instead. Pasties can be kept in the fridge for about 3 days and can be frozen for up to 3 months. To reheat, pop them in the microwave or heat them in the oven for a crispier crust.

Lean ground beef	2 lbs.	900 g
Diced onion	1 cup	250 mL
Diced potato	1 cup	250 mL
Chopped carrot	1 cup	250 mL
Kernel corn (optional)	1/2 cup	125 mL
Garlic cloves, minced	2	2
Salt	1 tsp.	5 mL
Pepper	1/2 tsp.	2 mL
All-purpose flour	2 2/3 cup	650 mL
Butter, unsalted	1 cup	250 mL
Salt	2 tsp.	10 mL
Water	3/4 cup	175 mL
Large eggs	2	2
Water	2 tbsp.	30 mL

Combine first 8 ingredients in a large bowl. Set aside.

Combine next 3 ingredients in a food processor and process into a crumb-like mixture. Gradually add water and process until dough becomes a smooth ball. Add more or less water if needed. Transfer dough to a work surface dusted with flour and divide into 8 equal portions. Roll each portion into an 8 inch round. Divide beef mixture equally among each round, leaving a 1/2 inch border around edge of dough. Fold over and press edges firmly shut. Place on a large greased bake sheet.

Combine eggs and second amount of water and brush over top of pastry. Press down edges with a fork. Bake in an 400°F (200°C) oven for 50 to 55 minutes or until golden brown. Makes 8 pasties.

Packing the lunch kit: Reheat pasties in the microwave or a 375°F (190°C) oven until warmed through and transfer to a warmed insulated container.

Brunch 'Wiches

This sandwich comes together quickly if you have the batch-cooking Breakfast Sausage (see p. 15) and oven omelette (see p. 14) on hand. Reheat the omelette and breakfast sausage in the microwave. If you do not have any omelette readily available, just use a fried egg in its place.

Cheddar cheese slice	1	1
Cooked breakfast sausage patty (see p. 15)	1	1
English muffin	1	1
Dijonnaise (see Tip, below)	1 tbsp.	15 mL
Oven omelette portion (see p. 19)	1	1

Reheat breakfast sausage in microwave until almost heated through. Add cheese slice and heat in microwave until cheese has melted.

Split English muffin and toast until golden. Spread bottom half with dijonnaise. Top with egg and breakfast sausage. Cover with remaining half of English muffin. Makes 1 sandwich.

Packing the lunch kit: Place warm sandwich in a warmed insulated container.

Tip: You can find dijonnaise at your local supermarket where the mayonnaise is kept, or make your own by combining about 1 tbsp. (15 mL) Dijon mustard with 1/2 cup (125 mL) mayo.

Pizza Pockets

Your kids' eyes will light up when they see one of these tasty, hand-held pizza pockets in their lunchbox. These pockets will keep for about 3 days in the fridge, and they freeze beautifully for up to 3 months.

Cooking oil	2 tsp.	10 mL
Chopped fresh white mushrooms	1 cup	250 mL
Chopped green pepper	1/2 cup	125 mL
Chopped onion	1/2 cup	125 mL
Dried crushed chilies (optional)	1/4 tsp.	1 mL
Pizza sauce	1/2 cup	125 mL
Grated Italian cheese blend	1 1/2 cups	375 mL
Sliced deli pepperoni sticks (1/4 inch, 6 mm, thick)	3/4 cup	175 mL
Large egg, lightly beaten	1	1
Water	1 tbsp.	15 mL
Frozen white bread dough, covered, thawed in refrigerator overnight	1	1

Heat cooking oil in a medium frying pan on medium. Add next 4 ingredients. Cook for about 8 minutes, stirring occasionally, until onion is softened. Remove from heat.

Stir in pizza sauce and transfer to a medium bowl. Let stand for 10 minutes.

Add cheese and pepperoni. Stir well.

Combine egg and water in a small bowl. Divide dough into 8 equal portions. Roll out 1 portion on a lightly floured surface to a 6 inch (15 cm) diameter circle. Spoon about 1/4 cup (60 mL) filling on half of circle, leaving 1/2 inch (12 mm) edge. Brush edge of dough with egg mixture. Fold dough over pepperoni mixture. Crimp edges with a fork or pinch together to seal. Repeat with remaining dough and pepperoni mixture. Arrange about 2 inches (5 cm) apart on a greased baking sheet. Brush with remaining egg mixture. Cut 2 or 3 small slits in tops to allow steam to escape. Bake in 375°F (190°C) oven for about 22 minutes until golden. Makes 8 pizza pockets.

Packing the lunch box: Reheat pizza pocket in toaster oven or microwave until warmed through, then transfer to a warmed insulated container.

Simple Croque Monsieur

Elevate the traditional grilled cheese into something extraordinary! This sandwich comes together quickly if you have some of the batch-cooking French Toast (see p. 20) on hand. If you want to make it the night before, store it in an airtight container in the fridge and reheat it in a toaster oven or oven until the bread is crispy. It is also freezable, so you can make a double batch and toss the extras in the freezer, individually wrapped.

Grated Italian cheese blend	3/4 cup	175 mL
French toast slices (see p. 20)	6	6
Deli ham slices, halved	3	3
Butter	2 tsp.	10 mL

Sprinkle half of cheese on 3 toast slices. Place ham slices over top and sprinkle with remaining cheese. Top with remaining bread slices.

Heat butter in a large frying pan on medium. Cook sandwiches until golden, about 3 to 5 minutes. Flip sandwiches and cook other side until golden. Makes 3 sandwiches.

Packing the lunch kit: Reheat sandwiches in microwave or, for a crisper crust, in toaster oven until warmed through. Cut in half and transfer to a warmed insulated container.

Cheese-wrapped Dogs

Kids will love the crunchy cornmeal pastry that makes these hot dogs extra special. This is another great recipe to make ahead and freeze. Wrapped individually with plastic wrap, the hot dogs will keep in the freezer for up to 3 months. Reheat from frozen in the oven, toaster oven or microwave.

All-purpose flour	1 1/4 cups	300 mL
Yellow cornmeal	1/4 cup	60 mL
Baking powder	1 tbsp.	15 mL
Cold hard butter (or margarine), cut up	1/3 cup	75 mL
Milk	1/2 cup	125 mL
Wieners (your favourite)	6	6
Grated medium (or mild) Cheddar cheese	3/4 cup	175 mL

Combine first 3 ingredients in a medium bowl. Cut in margarine until mixture resembles coarse crumbs. Make a well in centre.

Add milk to well. Stir until just moistened. Turn out dough onto a lightly floured surface. Knead 5 or 6 times. Roll out or press into a 12 inch (30 cm) square. Cut in half, and cut each half into 3 equal portions, for a total of 6.

Place 1 wiener lengthwise down centre of 1 dough portion. Sprinkle 2 tbsp. (30 mL) cheese evenly over top. Fold both long sides over wiener. Pinch together to seal. Repeat with remaining dough portions, wieners and cheese. Arrange rolls, seam-side down, evenly spaced apart on a greased baking sheet. Bake in 425°F (220°C) oven for 12 to 15 minutes until golden. Makes 6 hot dogs.

Packing the lunch kit: For a crispier crust, reheat hot dogs in an oven or toaster until warmed through. For a softer crust, reheat in microwave. Transfer to a warmed insulated container.

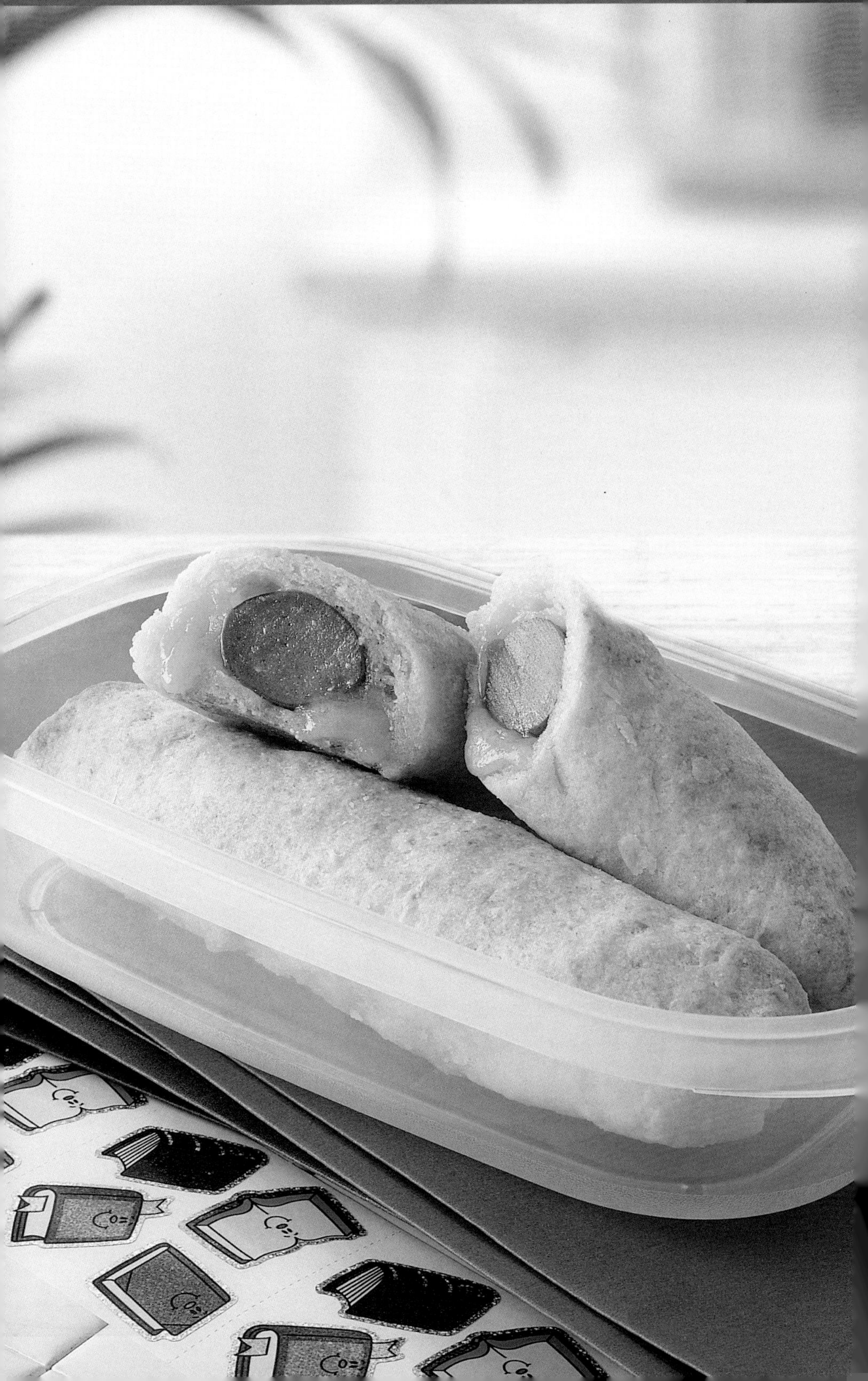

Chicken Waffle Sandwiches

This sandwich is delicious made with regular waffles, but for a special treat try the cheesy waffle variation (see p. 21). If you don't have time to make the chicken fingers for this recipe, use the Seasoned Chicken Strips (see p. 16), or even the Chicken Nuggets (see p. 44) instead. For best results, make the waffles and chicken fingers in advance and assemble the sandwich in the morning. Reheat the waffles before spreading them with the honey mustard mayo.

Panko bread crumbs	1 1/2 cups	375 mL
Ground sage	1/2 tsp.	2 mL
Dried oregano	1/2 tsp.	2 mL
Dried thyme	1/4 tsp.	1 mL
Salt	1/4 tsp.	1 mL
All-purpose flour	1/2 cup	125 mL
Large eggs, lightly beaten	2	2
Milk	3 tbsp.	45 mL
Skinless, boneless chicken breast halves, cut into 1 inch (2.5 cm) slices lengthwise	1 lb.	454 g
Mayonnaise	1/2 cup	125 mL
Dijon mustard	2 tsp.	10 mL
Liquid honey	2 tbsp.	30 mL
Lemon juice	2 tsp.	10 mL
Pepper	1/2 tsp.	2 mL
Romaine lettuce leaves	4	4
Thinly sliced cucumber	1 cup	250 mL
Waffles (see p. 21)	8	8

Combine first 5 ingredients in a large resealable freezer bag. Place flour in a shallow dish.

Combine eggs and milk in a separate shallow dish. Press one piece of chicken into flour to coat. Dip chicken piece into egg mixture and drop into resealable bag. Seal bag and shake until chicken is coated. Transfer chicken piece to a greased baking sheet. Repeat process until all chicken fingers have been coated. Discard any remaining flour, eggs and bread crumb mixture. Bake chicken fingers in 350°F (175°C) oven for 15 minutes until golden.

For the honey mustard mayonnaise, combine next 5 ingredients in a small bowl.

To make the sandwich, spread mayonnaise mixture on 4 waffles. Top each with lettuce, cucumbers and 2 or 3 chicken fingers. Place remaining 4 waffles on chicken fingers. Makes 4 sandwiches.

Packing the lunch kit: Reheat waffles and chicken fingers in oven or toaster oven until warmed through and crispy. Spread half of waffles with mayo mixture and top with lettuce, cucumbers, chicken fingers and remaining waffles. Transfer to a warmed insulated container.

Southwestern Chicken Wraps

This wrap can be made up to 2 days in advance and stored in the fridge. If you prefer to assemble the wrap in the morning, make the salsa the night before to give the flavours time to blend. Any leftover salsa can be stored in the fridge for 3 to 5 days.

Diced avocado	1 cup	250 mL
Can of kernel corn (7 oz., 199 mL), drained	1	1
Diced English cucumber (with peel)	1/2 cup	125 mL
Diced tomato	1/2 cup	125 mL
Thinly sliced green onion	3 tbsp.	45 mL
Lime juice	1 tbsp.	15 mL
Granulated sugar	1 tsp.	5 mL
Salt	1/4 tsp.	1 mL
Cooked, seasoned chicken (see p. 16)	2 cups	500 mL
Flour tortillas (9 inch, 23 cm, diameter)	4	4

For the salsa, combine first 8 ingredients in a medium bowl.

For the wraps, spoon salsa along centre of each tortilla and top with chicken, using 1/4 cup (60 mL) per wrap. Fold sides in and roll up from bottom to enclose. Cut each wrap in half. Makes 4 wraps.

Packing the lunch kit: Place wrap in an insulated lunch bag with a cooler pack to keep it cool.

Roasted Veggie Wraps

For this wrap, we've used the batch-cooking Roasted Veggies (see p. 18), but feel free to use your favourite combination of roasted veggies or whatever you have on hand. It takes very little time to assemble, but if your mornings are particularly rushed, you can always make it ahead and store it for up to 2 days in the fridge. The tomato will make the wrap watery if it sits too long. Do not freeze.

Mayonnaise	1/4 cup	60 mL
Lemon juice	2 tsp.	10 mL
Grainy Dijon mustard	2 tsp.	10 mL
Salt	1/4 tsp.	1 mL
Garlic powder	1/4 tsp.	1 mL
Spinach tortillas (9 inch, 23 cm, diameter)	4	4
Romaine lettuce leaves	4	4
Thin tomato slices	8	8
Roasted vegetables (see p. 18)	2 cups	500 mL
Grated Mozzarella cheese	2 cups	500 mL

Combine first 5 ingredients in a small bowl.

Spread mayonnaise mixture on tortillas. Layer 1 lettuce leaf, 2 tomato slices and 1/4 cup (60 mL) roasted veggies in order given over each tortilla. Sprinkle cheese over top, dividing cheese evenly between wraps. Fold bottom over filling, and then fold both sides in. Makes 4 wraps.

Packing the lunch kit: Transfer wrap to a container and place in an insulated lunch bag with a cooler pack.

Easy Cheesy Quesadillas

Feel free to customize the quesadillas by adding your child's favourite veggies or meat, or by switching up the cheese. If you are making only one or two quesadillas, you could pan fry instead them of baking them in the oven, if you prefer. The quesadillas can be made ahead and stored for about 2 days in the fridge, but the tomato will become watery the longer it sits.

Block cream cheese, softened	1/2 cup	125 mL
Flour tortillas (9 inch, 23 cm, diameter)	4	4
Grated Mexican cheese blend	1 1/2 cups	375 mL
Finely diced seeded tomato	1/2 cup	125 mL
Cooked black beans	1/2 cup	125 mL
Kernel corn	1/2 cup	125 mL

Spread cream cheese over each tortilla, almost to edge.

Sprinkle next 4 ingredients, in order given, over half of each tortilla. Fold tortillas in half to cover filling and press down lightly. Arrange on a greased a baking sheet with sides. Spray tortillas with cooking spray. Cook in 400°F (200°C) oven for about 15 minutes until crisp and cheese is melted. Each tortilla cuts into 4 wedges, for a total of 16 wedges.

Packing the lunch kit: For crispier wedges, reheat in an oven or toaster until warmed through. For a softer, chewier wedge, reheat in microwave. Transfer wedges to a warmed insulated container.

Skillet Lasagna

Ahh…the ultimate comfort food. This lasagna is cooked on the stovetop in a fraction of the time that traditional lasagna takes in the oven. Make sure you use a heavy weighted skillet. If the handle is not oven proof, cover it with foil before putting it into the oven. This dish is perfect for busy weeknights when the last thing you want to do in the evening is prepare a time-consuming meal. Make it for dinner and reheat portions in the morning for your family's lunches. This lasagna will keep in the fridge for 3 or 4 days.

Cottage cheese	1 1/2 cup	375 mL
Salt	1/2 tsp.	2 mL
Pepper	1/2 tsp.	2 mL
Dried oregano	1/2 tsp.	2 mL
Olive oil	1 tsp.	5 mL
Diced onion	3/4 cup	175 mL
Lean ground beef	1 lb.	454 g
Lasagna noodles, oven ready, broken into pieces	8	8
Tomato sauce	3 1/2 cups	875 mL
Water	1/2 cup	125 mL
Italian seasoning	1 1/2 tsp.	7 mL
Grated Mozzarella cheese	1 cup	250 mL
Grated Parmesan cheese	1/2 cup	125 mL

Combine first 4 ingredients in a small bowl. Set aside.

Heat olive oil in a large skillet on medium. Add onion and cook until translucent, about 4 to 5 minutes. Add ground beef and scrambled fry until meat is cooked through, about 8 to 10 minutes. Drain.

Scatter lasagna noodles over ground beef.

Combine next 3 ingredients in a medium bowl and spread over lasagna noodles, ensuring noodles are completely covered. Do not stir. Increase heat until sauce begins to simmer. Reduce heat to medium-low. Cook, covered, for about 10 minutes. Remove lid carefully and stir mixture. Cook, covered, for another 10 minutes, stirring occasionally to ensure noodles are not sticking to bottom. Add up to another 1/2 cup (125 mL) water, if needed.

Turn off heat. Dab cottage cheese mixture on top of noodle mixture. Let stand for 5 minutes, covered, to warm cheese. Carefully fold cottage cheese mixture into noodle mixture. Sprinkle with both remaining cheeses. Broil on centre rack for 2 to 3 minutes, until cheese is golden and bubbly. Makes 8 servings.

Packing the lunch kit: Reheat lasagna in microwave and transfer to a warmed insulated container.

Bacon and Pea Fusilli

This pasta dish makes a nice light lunch for anyone who doesn't like to eat a heavy meal in the middle of the day. It will last in the fridge for up to 3 days and reheats well in the microwave. If your young'uns love all things cheesy, stir a little grated Parmesan or mozzarella cheese into the warm pasta before transferring it to the warmed insulated container.

Water	8 cups	2 L
Salt	1 tsp.	5 mL
Fusilli pasta	1 1/2 cups	375 mL
Bacon slices, chopped	4	4
Thinly sliced leek (white part only)	1 cup	250 mL
Garlic clove, minced	1	1
(or 1/4 tsp., 1 mL, powder)		
Frozen peas	1 cup	250 mL
Grated lemon zest	1 tsp.	5 mL

Combine water and salt in a large saucepan and bring to a boil. Add pasta and cook, uncovered, for 7 to 9 minutes, stirring occasionally, until tender but firm. Drain, reserving 1/4 cup (60 mL) cooking water. Return to same pot. Cover to keep warm.

Combine next 3 ingredients in a large frying pan on medium. Cook, stirring occasionally, until leek is softened. Stir in peas and reserved cooking water. Bring to a boil and simmer for about 2 minutes until peas are tender. Toss in pasta.

Sprinkle with lemon zest and toss. Makes about 4 cups (1 L).

Packing the lunch kit: Reheat pasta in microwave and transfer to a warmed insulated container.

Chicken Pad Thai

If you don't have any cooked chicken, this recipe is just as delicious as a vegetarian dish. It can be stored in the fridge for up to 3 days, but we do not recommend freezing it because the noodles do not hold up well when thawed and reheated. Most versions of this dish contain bean sprouts, but there has been much debate about whether it is safe for children to eat bean sprouts that have not been well cooked, so we opted to use bamboo shoots instead. The peanuts add a nice crunch, but leave them out if your kid's school is nut free.

Medium rice stick noodles	1/2 lb.	225 g
Sesame (or cooking) oil	1 tbsp.	15 mL
Apricot jam	1/4 cup	60 mL
Lime juice	1/4 cup	60 mL
Soy sauce	3 tbsp.	45 mL
Cornstarch	1 tbsp.	15 mL
Chili paste (sambal oelek), optional	1/4 tsp.	1 mL
Pepper	1/2 tsp.	2 mL
Cooked, seasoned chicken (see p. 16)	2 cups	500 mL
Sliced bamboo shoots	1/2 cup	125 mL
Thinly sliced red pepper	1 cup	250 mL
Julienned carrots	1 cup	250 mL
Spinach, chopped	1 cup	250 mL
Unsalted peanuts, chopped (optional)	1/4 cup	60 mL
Chopped fresh cilantro (or parsley)	2 tbsp.	30 mL

Cover noodles with hot water in a medium bowl and let stand for about 30 minutes until soft. Drain and return to same bowl. Drizzle with sesame oil and toss lightly.

Stir next 6 ingredients in a small bowl until smooth. Heat in a medium frying pan, stirring constantly, until boiling and thickened. Add chicken and cook until chicken is warmed through. Add bamboo shoots, red pepper, carrots, spinach and noodles, and toss until coated.

Sprinkle individual servings with peanuts and cilantro. Makes 6 cups (1.5 L).

Packing the lunch kit: Reheat a portion in microwave until warmed through. Transfer to a warmed insulated serving container.

Sukiyaki Rice Bowl

This quick Japanese dish has become a perennial food-court favourite. But why fight the crowds at the mall when you can make it so easily, and so much better, at home? Serve over long grain white rice. The beef mixture can be made ahead and will keep in the fridge for 3 to 4 days. Cooked rice will keep for 3 to 4 days in the fridge and can be frozen for up 2 months.

Prepared beef broth	1/2 cup	125 mL
Cornstarch	2 tbsp.	30 mL
Low-sodium soy sauce	1/2 cup	125 mL
Apple juice	1/2 cup	125 mL
Granulated sugar	2 tbsp.	30 mL
Cooking oil	2 tsp.	10 mL
Lean ground beef	1 lb.	454 g
Cooking oil	2 tsp.	10 mL
Large onion, cut into thin wedges	1	1
Sliced fresh white mushrooms	1 1/2 cups	375 mL
Shredded Napa cabbage	2 cups	500 mL
Thinly sliced carrot	1 cup	250 mL
Can of bamboo shoots (8 oz., 227 mL), drained	1	1
Green onions, cut into 1 inch (2.5 cm) pieces	4	4

Stir broth into cornstarch in a small bowl. Stir in next 3 ingredients and set aside.

Heat a large frying pan or wok on medium. Add first amount of cooking oil. Add beef and stir-fry for about 10 minutes until no longer pink. Drain and transfer to a small bowl. Set aside.

Add second amount of cooking oil to hot frying pan. Add onion and mushrooms and stir-fry for 5 to 10 minutes, until onion is softened.

Add next 4 ingredients and stir-fry for 2 to 3 minutes until carrot is tender-crisp. Add beef. Stir cornstarch mixture and add to beef mixture. Heat, stirring, for 1 to 2 minutes until boiling and thickened. Makes 4 servings.

Packing the lunch kit: Reheat a portion of beef mixture and rice in microwave and transfer to a warmed insulated container.

Cauliflower Fried Rice

Love rice but want to provide your children with a little extra nutrition? Try this stir-fry, which uses riced cauliflower in place of the traditional white rice. This dish comes together so quickly that it can be made in the morning before the kids head out for school, but it can also be made in advance. Store it in the fridge for up to 3 days. It also freezes well.

Olive oil	1 tbsp.	15 mL
Diced carrot	1 cup	250 mL
Diced onion	1/2 cup	125 mL
Cauliflower rice (see Tip, below)	3 cups	750 mL
Kernel corn	3/4 cup	175 mL
Frozen peas, thawed	3/4 cup	175 mL
Garlic cloves, minced	2	2
Soy sauce	2 tbsp.	30 mL
Minced fresh ginger root	2 tsp.	10 mL
Brown sugar	2 tsp.	10 mL
Cornstarch	1 tsp.	5 mL
Dried crushed chilies	1/8 tsp.	0.5 mL

Heat a large frying pan or wok on medium-high until very hot. Add oil. Add carrots and onion and stir-fry for about 3 minutes, until carrots are soft.

Add next 4 ingredients and stir-fry for 3 to 5 minutes until vegetables are tender crisp.

Combine remaining 5 ingredients in a small cup. Add to cauliflower mixture and heat until boiling and thickened. Makes 6 servings.

Packing the lunch kit: If making in advance, reheat cauliflower fried rice in the microwave. Transfer to a warmed insulated container.

Tip: Look for cauliflower rice in the frozen section of your local supermarket. If you prefer to make your own, remove all greens and woodsy parts of stems from a head of cauliflower and cut it into 4 pieces. Wash and dry cauliflower pieces thoroughly. Grate cauliflower using the medium-size holes you would use for cheese, or use the grater attachment of a food processor and pulse the cauliflower into small pieces. Transfer the cauliflower pieces to paper towels or an absorbent tea towel to remove any extra water. It is then ready to be used in your recipe.

Chicken Vegetable Fried Rice

With veggies, chicken and ham, this great mix is sure to be popular with the kids. You can either prepare the meat and veggies in advance and toss them in a frying pan with the rice in the morning to warm the dish up, or prepare the entire dish the night before and reheat it in the microwave in the morning. This stir-fry will keep in the fridge for about 3 days.

Cooking oil	1 tbsp.	15 mL
Boneless, skinless chicken breast halves, thinly sliced	3/4 lb.	340 g
Chopped green pepper	1 cup	250 mL
Chopped red pepper	1 cup	250 mL
Frozen peas	1 cup	250 mL
Can of sliced water chestnuts (8 oz., 227 mL), drained	1	1
Thinly sliced green onion	1/2 cup	125 mL
Chopped low-fat deli ham	1/2 cup	125 mL
Low-sodium soy sauce	1 1/2 tbsp.	25 mL
Hoisin sauce	1 tbsp.	15 mL
Sweet chili sauce (optional)	1 tbsp.	15 mL
Cold cooked long grain white rice (about 2/3 cup, 150 mL, uncooked)	2 cups	500 mL

Heat a wok or large frying pan on medium-high until very hot. Add cooking oil and chicken, and stir-fry for 3 to 5 minutes until chicken is no longer pink.

Add next 6 ingredients. Stir-fry for 2 to 3 minutes until peppers are tender-crisp.

Combine next 3 ingredients in a small bowl. Add to chicken mixture and stir well.

Add rice. Stir-fry for about 5 minutes until heated through and liquid is almost evaporated. Makes 6 servings.

Packing the lunch kit: Transfer a portion of warm stir-fry to a warmed insulated container.

Tunisian Couscous

If the idea of more rice or potatoes is boring your kids to tears, make them this exotic couscous instead. It can be made in advance and stored in the fridge in an airtight container for up to 3 days. Do not freeze. We prefer this dish warm, but it is also delicious cold.

Water	1 3/4 cups	425 mL
Salt	1/4 tsp.	1 mL
Couscous	1 cup	250 mL
Olive (or cooking) oil	1 tbsp.	15 mL
Chopped onion	1 cup	250 mL
Finely diced carrot	1/4 cup	60 mL
Diced red pepper	1/2 cup	125 mL
Frozen peas	1/2 cup	125 mL
Brown sugar, packed	1 tsp.	5 mL
Ground cumin	1/2 tsp.	2 mL
Montreal steak spice	1/2 tsp.	2 mL
Garlic clove, minced	1	1
(or 1/4 tsp., 1 mL, powder)		
Ground cinnamon	1/4 tsp.	1 mL
Cayenne pepper	1/8 tsp.	0.5 mL
Lemon juice	2 tbsp.	30 mL

Combine water and salt in a small saucepan and bring to a boil. Stir in couscous and remove from heat. Let stand, covered, for 5 minutes. Fluff with a fork. Cover and set aside.

Meanwhile, heat olive oil in a large frying pan on medium. Add onion and carrot. Cook for about 5 minutes, stirring often, until onion is softened.

Add next 8 ingredients. Cook for about 3 minutes, stirring often, until garlic is fragrant and carrot is tender.

Stir in lemon juice and couscous. Makes about 4 cups (1 L).

Packing the lunch kit: For warm couscous, reheat a portion in microwave and transfer to a warmed insulated container. For cold couscous, pack it in an airtight container and place it in an insulated lunch bad with a cooler pack.

Italian Meatball Soup

This soup is really quick to prepare, especially if you use meatballs that are not frozen. If you are ambitious in the morning, you could make it before you head out the door to start your day. However, most of us would probably prefer to prepare it the night before and simply reheat it in the microwave in the morning. We've used space-shaped pasta, but any small pasta, such as orzo or alphabet, would work just as well. This soup will keep in the fridge for 3 to 4 days. You can freeze it, but the pasta will absorb the liquid and be much softer when the soup is reheated.

Prepared beef broth	7 cups	1.75 L
Very small pasta (such as orzo or shaped pasta)	2/3 cup	150 mL
Meatballs (see p. 14)	65	65
Finely shredded fresh basil	2 tbsp.	30 mL

In a large pot or Dutch oven, bring broth to a boil on high. Stir in pasta and reduce heat to medium. Boil gently, uncovered, for 5 to 6 minutes until pasta is tender but firm.

Add meatballs and basil. Heat, stirring, until meatballs are heated through. Makes about 8 cups (2 L).

Packing the lunch kit: Transfer a portion of warm soup to a warmed insulated container.

Chicken Zoodle Soup

Using your favourite prepared chicken broth (homemade or store bought) and cooked chicken such as the batch-cooking Seasonal Chicken Strips (see p. 16) really cuts down the amount of time needed to prepare this soup. Replacing half of the egg noodles with zucchini noodles is a fun way to get extra vegetables into your kids' diet. This soup will keep in the fridge for 3 to 4 days but does not freeze well.

Cooking oil	2 tsp.	10 mL
Chopped onion	1/2 cup	125 mL
Chopped carrot	1/2 cup	125 mL
Chopped celery	1/2 cup	125 mL
Prepared chicken broth	8 cups	2 L
Egg noodles	1 1/2 cups	375 mL
Zucchini noodles (see Tip, below)	3 cups	750 mL
Chopped cooked chicken (see p. 16)	1 1/2 cups	375 mL
Chopped fresh parsley	1/4 cup	60 mL
Salt	3/4 tsp.	4 mL
Pepper	1/4 tsp.	1 mL

Heat cooking oil in a large saucepan on medium. Add next 3 ingredients and cook for 5 to 10 minutes, stirring often, until onion is softened. Add broth and bring to a boil.

Add egg noodles and cook, uncovered, for about 10 minutes, stirring occasionally, until noodles and vegetables are tender.

Add zucchini noodles, chicken, parsley, salt and pepper. Heat, stirring, until chicken is heated through. Makes about 10 cups (2.5 L).

Packing the lunch kit: Reheat a portion of soup in microwave or on stovetop and transfer to a warmed insulated container.

Tip: If you don't have a spiralizer or mandolin to cut your zucchini into noodles, you can use a vegetable peeler instead but your noodles with be thicker. Prepared zucchini noodles can also be found in the produce or refrigeration section of many supermarkets.

Autumn Pumpkin Soup

This is another easy soup that comes together quickly, in about 30 minutes, so you can make it in the morning before you head out, if you are so inclined. It can also be made in advance stored in the fridge for 3 to 5 days or in the freezer for up to 2 months.

Olive (or cooking) oil	2 tsp.	10 mL
Chopped onion	1 1/2 cups	375 mL
Low-sodium prepared chicken (or vegetable) broth	4 cups	1 L
Can of pure pumpkin (no spices) (14 oz., 398 mL)	1	1
Unsweetened applesauce	1 cup	250 mL
Bay leaf	1	1
Chopped fresh thyme (or 1/2 tsp., 2 mL, dried)	2 tsp.	10 mL
Lemon pepper	1 tsp.	5 mL
Salt, to taste		

Heat olive oil in a large saucepan on medium. Add onion and cook for 5 to 10 minutes, stirring occasionally, until softened and starting to brown.

Stir in remaining 7 ingredients and bring to a boil. Reduce heat to medium-low and simmer, partially covered, for 10 minutes to blend flavours. Discard bay leaf. Makes about 7 cups (1.75 L).

Packing the lunch kit: Transfer a portion of warm soup to a warmed insulated container.

BLT Pasta Salad

This salad can be made the night before and stored in the fridge, but make sure you pack the dressing separate from the salad to keep the salad fresh and prevent it from going soggy.

Ingredient	Imperial	Metric
Thick plain yogurt (see Tip, p. 62)	1/2 cup	125 mL
Lemon juice	1 tsp.	5 mL
Apple cider vinegar	1/2 tsp.	2 mL
Dried dill weed	1/2 tsp.	2 mL
Dried parsley	1/2 tsp.	2 mL
Garlic powder	1/4 tsp.	1 mL
Onion powder	1/4 tsp.	1 mL
Salt	1/4 tsp.	1 mL
Pepper	1/8 tsp.	0.5 mL
Cooked farfalle pasta	4 cups	1 L
Grape tomatoes, cut in half	1 1/2 cups	375 mL
Cooked bacon slices, crumbled	6	6
Grated Cheddar cheese	1 cup	250 mL
Sliced green onion	1/4 cup	60 mL
Cut or torn romaine lettuce	4 cups	1 L

For the dressing, combine first 9 ingredients in a small bowl. Makes about 1/2 cup (125 mL).

For the salad, combine next 5 ingredients in a large bowl. Sprinkle lettuce on top of the pasta mixture. When you are ready to eat, add dressing and toss lightly to coat. Makes 6 servings.

Packing the lunch kit: Transfer a portion of salad to a container and place in an insulated lunch bag with a cooler pack. Transfer a portion of dressing to a leakproof container and add to lunch kit.

At lunchtime, pour dressing over salad and toss to coat.

Chicken Taco Salad

You can prepare the chicken and salad in advance, but for best results prepare the avocado and tomato in the morning and add them just before you transfer the salad to the lunch container. If you don't have time to prepare the chicken as directed below, feel free to use the batch-cooking Seasoned Chicken Strips (see p. 16) or even the Chili (see p. 12) instead. Pack a few tortilla chips on the side.

Canola oil	1 tsp.	5 mL
Extra-lean ground chicken breast	3/4 lb.	340 g
Chili powder	2 tsp.	10 mL
Ground cumin	1/2 tsp.	2 mL
Garlic powder	1/4 tsp.	1 mL
Salsa	1/4 cup	60 mL
Cut or torn romaine lettuce, lightly packed	8 cups	2 L
Canned black beans, drained and rinsed	1 cup	250 mL
Slivered red pepper	1 cup	250 mL
Thinly sliced red onion	1/2 cup	125 mL
Light sour cream	1/4 cup	60 mL
Salsa	1/4 cup	60 mL
Lime juice	2 tbsp.	30 mL
Granulated sugar	1/2 tsp.	2 mL
Diced avocado	1 cup	250 mL
Diced tomato	1 cup	250 mL
Chopped fresh cilantro (or parsley)	2 tbsp.	30 mL

Heat canola oil in a large frying pan on medium. Add next 4 ingredients and scramble-fry for about 8 minutes until chicken is no longer pink. Stir in first amount of salsa. Remove from heat and let stand for 10 minutes.

Toss next 4 ingredients in a large bowl.

Stir next 4 ingredients in a small bowl until smooth. Add to lettuce mixture and toss well.

Add remaining 3 ingredients and chicken mixture and toss lightly. Makes about 13 cups (3.25 L).

Packing the lunch kit: Transfer a portion of salad to a container and place in an insulated lunch bag with a cooler pack.

Mango Chicken Salad

If you plan to make this salad in advance, toss the avocado in a little lemon juice to prevent it from going brown. The batch-cooking Seasoned Chicken Strips (see p. 16) are excellent in this salad if you have any on hand in the fridge but do not use them if they were previously frozen. Store the dressing separately from the salad.

Cut or torn romaine lettuce	8 cups	2 L
Large mango, peeled, seeded and chopped	1	1
Medium English cucumber, sliced	1	1
Diced avocado	1/2 cup	125 mL
Chopped cooked seasoned chicken (see p. 16)	2 cups	500 mL
Olive oil	2 tbsp	30 mL
Liquid honey	2 tbsp.	30 mL
Orange juice	2 tbsp.	30 mL
White balsamic vinegar	2 tbsp.	30 mL
Grated orange zest (see Tip, below)	1 1/2 tsp.	7 mL
Salt	1/4 tsp.	1 mL
Pepper, to taste		

Combine first 5 ingredients in a large bowl.

Combine remaining 7 ingredients in a jar with a tight-fitting lid and shake until well combined. Pour over salad mixture and toss until well coated. Makes 6 servings.

Packing the lunch kit: Transfer a portion of salad to a cooled insulated container or place in a regular container in an insulated lunch bag with a cooler pack. Pour a serving of dressing into a leakproof container and pack in insulated lunch bag.

At lunchtime, drizzle dressing over salad and toss lightly so everything is evenly coated with dressing.

Tip: When a recipe calls for grated zest and juice, it's easier to grate the fruit first, then juice it. Be careful not to grate down to the pith (white part of the peel), which is bitter and best avoided.

Soba Noodle Salad

What kid doesn't love noodles? Loaded with veggies and chicken, this salad is substantial enough to keep your little ones full throughout the afternoon. It can be made in advance and stored in the fridge for up to 3 days. Do not freeze.

Soy sauce	2 tbsp.	30 mL
Rice vinegar	1 tbsp.	15 mL
Lime juice	1 tbsp.	15 mL
Liquid honey	1 tsp.	5 mL
Olive oil	1 tsp.	5 mL
Cold cooked soba noodles	1 cup	250 mL
Chopped broccoli	1/4 cup	60 mL
Diced red pepper	1/4 cup	60 mL
Diced yellow pepper	1/4 cup	60 mL
Chopped cooked seasoned chicken (see p. 16)	1 cup	250 mL
Chopped green onion	3 tbsp.	45 mL
Sesame seeds	2 tbsp.	30 mL

For the dressing, combine first 5 ingredients in a jar with a tight-fitting lid and shake until well combined.

Combine next 5 ingredients in a large bowl, tossing gently. Drizzle dressing over top and toss lightly until everything is evenly coated with dressing.

Sprinkle with green onion and sesame seeds. Makes 2 servings.

Packing the lunch kit: Transfer a portion of salad to a cooled insulated container or place in a regular container in an insulated lunch bag with a cooler pack.

Lemon Potato Salad

All the flavours of lemony Greek potatoes in a salad form, and with bacon! This dish can be made in advance and stored in the fridge for 2 to 3 days. Do not freeze as the potatoes will be mushy once thawed. It can be eaten warm or cold.

Baby potatoes, halved	24	24
Small red onion, cut into 12 wedges (root intact)	1	1
Garlic cloves, minced	2	2
Olive (or cooking) oil	1/3 cup	75 mL
Lemon juice	3 tbsp.	45 mL
Dried oregano	2 tsp.	10 mL
Salt	1 1/2 tsp.	7 mL
Coarsely ground pepper	1 1/2 tsp.	7 mL
Grated lemon zest (see Tip, page 126)	1 tsp.	5 mL
Bacon slice, chopped	4	4
Thinly sliced celery	1 cup	250 mL
Thinly sliced green onion	1/4 cup	125 mL
Extra virgin olive oil	1/4 cup	60 mL
Lemon juice	2 tbsp.	30 mL
Chopped fresh oregano	1 tbsp.	15 mL
Liquid honey	1 tbsp.	15 mL
Grated lemon zest	2 tsp.	10 mL
Dijon mustard	1 tsp.	5 mL
Salt	1/4 tsp.	1 mL
Pepper	1/8 tsp.	0.5 mL

Arrange potato, onion and garlic in a 9 x 13 (23 x 33 cm) baking dish.

Combine next 6 ingredients in a small bowl. Drizzle over potato mixture. Bake in 375°F (190°C) oven for 30 minutes. Stir potatoes and cook for another 10 to 15 minutes, until potatoes are tender. Remove from oven and set aside to cool.

Meanwhile, cook bacon in a medium pan on medium. Transfer to a plate lined with paper towel to drain.

Chop red onion into pieces and transfer to a large bowl. Add potatoes, celery, bacon and green onion. Toss lightly.

Combine remaining 8 ingredients in a small bowl. Drizzle over potato salad and mix well. Makes 6 servings.

Packing the lunch kit:
For a cold salad,
transfer a portion
of salad to a cooled
insulated container
or use a regular
container and place it
in an insulated lunch
bag with a cooler
pack. For a warm
salad, reheat salad
in microwave and
transfer to a warmed
insulated container.

Berry Spinach Salad

If fresh strawberries are in season, they would also be delicious in this light, refreshing salad. For best results when you make the salad ahead, store the feta and dressing separately and add them at the last minute.

Olive (or cooking) oil	3 tbsp.	45 mL
Balsamic vinegar	2 tbsp.	30 mL
Strawberry jam, warmed	2 tbsp.	30 mL
Pepper	1/8 tsp.	0.5 mL
Fresh spinach leaves, lightly packed	10 cups	2.5 L
Fresh raspberries	1 1/4 cups	300 mL
Crumbled feta cheese (about 3 oz., 85 g)	2/3 cup	150 mL
Slivered almonds, toasted (see Tip, below)	1/2 cup	125 mL

For the dressing, combine first 4 ingredients in a jar with a tight-fitting lid. Shake until well combined. Set aside.

Combine remaining 4 ingredients in a large bowl, tossing gently. Drizzle dressing over salad and toss gently. Makes 8 servings.

Packing the lunch kit: Transfer a portion of salad to a cooled insulated container or use a regular container and place it in an insulated lunch kit. Pack feta and dressing in separate containers and place in insulated lunch kit.

At lunchtime, pour dressing over salad and sprinkle with feta. Toss lightly until everything is evenly coated with dressing.

Tip: When toasting nuts, seeds or coconut, cooking times will vary for each type of nut, so never toast them together. For small amounts, place the ingredient in an ungreased shallow frying pan. Heat on medium for 3 to 5 minutes, stirring often, until golden. For larger amounts, spread the ingredient evenly in an ungreased shallow pan. Bake in 350°F (175°C) oven for 5 to 10 minutes, stirring or shaking often, until golden.

Paradise Salad

Add a little tropical flair to your child's lunch with this tasty salad. You can use the batch-cooking Seasoned Chicken Strips (see p. 16) in this recipe if you have any on hand in the fridge but do not use it if it has been previously frozen. Prepare this salad ahead and store it in the fridge for about 2 days. For best results, store the dressing separately from the remaining salad ingredients, and prepare and add the avocado in the morning before transferring the salad to individual containers. The longer the avocado sits, the browner and softer it will become.

Extra virgin olive oil	1/4 cup	60 mL
Thick plain yogurt (see Tip, p. 62)	2 tbsp.	30 mL
Lemon juice	1 tbsp.	15 mL
Poppy seeds	1 tbsp.	15 mL
Liquid honey	2 tsp.	10 mL
Salt	1/4 tsp.	1 mL
Chopped lettuce	6 cups	1.5 L
Chopped pineapple	1 cup	250 mL
Canned mandarin orange slices, drained	1 cup	250 mL
Toasted medium coconut (see Tip, p. 132)	3 tbsp.	45 mL
Chopped cooked chicken (see p. 16)	2 cups	500 mL
Lemon juice	2 tbsp.	30 mL
Large avocado, chopped	1	1

Add first 6 ingredients to a jar with a tight-fitting lid and shake until well combined.

Combine next 7 ingredients in a large bowl and toss lightly. Drizzle with dressing and toss lightly until everything is well coated with dressing. Makes 6 servings.

Packing the lunch kit: Transfer a portion of salad to a cooled insulated container or use a regular container and place it in an insulated lunch bag with a cooler pack. Pour a portion of dressing into a leakproof container and add to insulated lunch kit.

Sausage and Cheese Biscuits

These biscuits make a great breakfast on the go or a light lunch for kids who are too busy socializing at lunchtime to eat a big lunch. The biscuits will keep in the fridge for 3 or 4 days and can be frozen for about 2 months. They can be eaten hot or cold.

Cooking oil	1 tsp.	5 mL
Breakfast sausage, casing removed	1/2 lb.	225 g
Finely chopped onion	1/2 cup	125 mL
Pepper	1/4 tsp.	1 mL
All-purpose flour	2 cups	500 mL
Baking powder	2 tsp.	10 mL
Baking soda	1/2 tsp.	2 mL
Salt	1/2 tsp.	2 mL
Cold butter (or hard margarine), cut up	1/4 cup	60 mL
Grated Cheddar cheese	1 cup	250 mL
Buttermilk (or soured milk, see Tip, page 24)	3/4 cup	175 mL
Milk	1 tbsp.	15 mL

Heat cooking oil in a large frying pan on medium-high. Add next 3 ingredients. Scramble-fry for about 5 minutes until sausage is browned. Drain.

Combine next 4 ingredients in a large bowl. Cut in butter until mixture resembles coarse crumbs. Stir in sausage mixture and cheese. Make a well in centre.

Add buttermilk to well. Stir until a soft dough forms. Turn out onto a lightly floured surface and knead 8 times. Roll or pat out to an 8 inch (20 cm) square. Cut into 4 inch (10 cm) squares. Cut each square in half to form triangles. Arrange on a greased baking sheet with sides.

Brush tops with milk. Bake in 425°F (220°C) oven for about 10 minutes until wooden pick inserted in centre of biscuit comes out clean. Let stand on baking sheet for 5 minutes before transferring to a wire rack to cool. Makes about 8 biscuits.

Packing the lunch kit: For a warm biscuit, reheat in microwave or toaster oven until warmed through and transfer to a warmed insulated container. If you are not warming the biscuit in advance, pack it in a container and place it in an insulated lunch bag with a cooler pack.

Breakfast Cookies

No need to feel guilty about packing these cookies in your child's lunch box! With no added fat or sugar, these moist morsels are more like a solid, hand-held bowl of oatmeal than a cookie. Oats, walnuts, dates, banana—there is not one unhealthy ingredient in the mix! A perfect snack for kids who aren't big breakfast or lunch eaters. Store in an airtight container for up to a week, or freeze for up to 3 months.

Ripe bananas	3	3
Rolled oats	2 cups	500 mL
Dates, pitted and chopped	1 cup	250 mL
Unsweetened applesauce	1/3 cup	75 mL
Vanilla extract	1 tsp.	5 mL
Ground cinnamon	1 tsp.	5 mL
Chopped walnuts	1/4 cup	60 mL
Dried cranberries (optional)	1/2 cup	125 mL

Mash bananas in a large bowl. Stir in oats, dates, applesauce, vanilla, cinnamon, walnuts and cranberries. Mix well and allow to sit for 15 minutes. Drop by teaspoonfuls onto an ungreased cookie sheet. Bake in 350°F (175°C) oven for about 20 minutes, until lightly brown. Makes 14 cookies.

Packing the lunch kit: No special instructions for these cookies. Just use a regular container.

Super Fruit Pizza

A great make-ahead treat that will make your kids' lunchbox the envy of the classroom. Any fruit can be used for the toppings, but we've opted for a combination of berries, kiwi and cantaloupe. The pizza will keep in the fridge for about 3 days. Do not freeze.

95% fat-free spreadable cream cheese	1 cup	250 mL
Granulated sugar	1/4 cup	60 mL
Vanilla extract	1/2 tsp.	2 mL
All-purpose flour	1 1/4 cups	300 mL
Quick-cooking rolled oats	1 cup	250 mL
Granulated sugar	1/3 cup	75 mL
Butter, melted	1/3 cup	75 mL
Canola oil	3 tbsp.	45 mL
Cantaloupe slices	1 cup	250 mL
Fresh strawberries, cut in half	1 cup	250 mL
Kiwi, skin removed, sliced	3/4 cup	175mL
Fresh blueberries	1/2 cup	125 mL
Fresh raspberries	1/3 cup	75 mL
Sliced almonds, toasted (see Tip, page 132), optional	1/4 cup	60 mL

Beat first 3 ingredients in a small bowl until smooth. Chill, covered, until ready to use.

Combine next 5 ingredients in a medium bowl until mixture resembles coarse crumbs. Press evenly into a greased 12 inch (30 cm) pizza pan. Bake in 350°F (175°C) oven for about 15 minutes until golden. Let stand on a wire rack until cool. Spread cream cheese mixture over crust, almost to edge.

Arrange next 5 ingredients over top. Sprinkle with almonds, if using. Cuts into 16 wedges.

Packing the lunch kit: Place a slice of fruit pizza in a container and place it in an insulated lunch bag with a cooler pack.

Guacamole Muffins

Any kid who likes Tex-Mex flavours will love this muffin. It tastes like corn chips dipped in guacamole! These muffins freeze well, so make a double batch and toss half of them into the freezer for up to 3 months.

All-purpose flour	2 cups	500 mL
Yellow cornmeal	1 cup	250 mL
Granulated sugar	2 tbsp.	30 mL
Baking powder	2 tsp.	10 mL
Baking soda	1 tsp.	5 mL
Salt	1/2 tsp.	2 mL
Large egg	1	1
Mashed avocado	1 cup	250 mL
Medium salsa	1/2 cup	125 mL
Milk	1/3 cup	75 mL
Butter (or hard margarine), melted	1/4 cup	60 mL
Lime juice	1 tbsp.	15 mL

Combine first 6 ingredients in a large bowl. Make a well in centre.

Combine remaining 6 ingredients in a medium bowl. Add to well and stir until just combined. Fill 12 greased muffin cups full. Bake in 375°F (190°C) oven for 20 to 22 minutes until wooden pick inserted in centre of muffin comes out clean. Let stand in pan for 5 minutes before removing to a wire rack to cool. Makes 12 muffins.

Packing the lunch kit: No special instructions needed for these muffins. Just pack them in a regular container.

Lemon Blueberry Loaf

*We've added a crunchy streusel topping to this lemon loaf, but if your kids'
school doesn't allow nuts, use the lemon glaze (see Tip, below) instead.*

All-purpose flour	2 cups	500 mL
Baking powder	1 1/4 tsp.	6 mL
Salt	1/2 tsp.	2 mL
Butter (or hard margarine), softened	1/2 cup	125 mL
Granulated sugar	1 cup	250 mL
Large eggs	3	3
Milk	1/2 cup	125 mL
Fresh (or frozen) blueberries	1 cup	250 mL
Grated lemon zest	1 1/2 tbsp.	22 mL
Finely chopped walnuts	1/4 cup	60 mL
Brown sugar, packed	2 tbsp.	30 mL
Ground cinnamon	1/4 tsp.	1 mL

Combine first 3 ingredients in a medium bowl. Set aside.

Cream butter and sugar in a large bowl. Add eggs 1 at a time, beating well
after each addition.

Add flour mixture in 3 parts, alternating with milk in 2 parts, stirring after
each addition until just combined. Fold in blueberries and lemon zest. Stir
until just combined. Spread in a greased 9 x 5 x 3 inch (23 x 12.5 x 7.5 cm)
loaf pan.

Combine remaining 3 ingredients in a small bowl. Sprinkle on batter. Bake
in 325°F (160°C) oven for about 1 hour until wooden pick inserted in centre
comes out clean. Let stand in pan for about 10 minutes before removing to
a wire rack to cool. Cuts into 16 slices.

Tip: To add a glaze to this loaf, combine 1/4 cup (60 mL) lemon juice and
1/4 cup (60 mL) icing (confectioner's) sugar in a small bowl, stirring until
smooth. Randomly poke several holes in loaf with wooden pick. Spoon
lemon juice mixture over hot loaf. Let stand in pan until cooled completely.

Packing the lunch kit: No special instructions needed for this loaf. Just pack
a slice in a regular container.

<![CDATA[

Granola Bars

Granola bars can be a healthy, portable snack, perfect for the lunch bag or as an after-school snack, but many that are available on supermarket shelves are full of unhealthy ingredients. Our version is loaded fibre-rich oats, almond butter for protein and dried cranberries and white chocolate chips for an added touch of sweetness. If your school does not allow almond butter, use sunflower seed butter instead.

Quick oats	1 1/2 cups	375 mL
Crisp rice cereal	1 1/2 cups	375 mL
Dried cranberries, chopped	1/3 cup	75 mL
White chocolate chips (see Note, below)	1/3 cup	75 mL
Ground cinnamon	1/2 tsp.	2 mL
Almond butter	1/2 cup	125 mL
Liquid honey	1/3 cup	75 mL
Coconut oil	1 tbsp.	15 mL
Vanilla extract	1 tsp.	5 mL

Combine first 5 ingredients in a large bowl. Set aside.

Grease or line an 8 x 8 inch (20 x 20 cm) pan with parchment paper. Set aside. Combine next 3 ingredients in a small saucepan on medium heat. Heat, stirring, until coconut oil has melted and mixture is well combined. Remove from heat and stir in vanilla. Pour over oat mixture and stir until well combined. Press mixture into prepared pan and press down firmly. Let stand until completely cool before cutting into bars. Cuts into 16 bars.

Packing the lunch kit: No special instructions needed for these granola bars. Just pack them in a regular container.

Note: If you add the white chocolate chips before adding the almond butter mixture, the heat from the almond butter mixture will melt the chocolate chips somewhat and the melted white chocolate will be distributed throughout the granola bar as you stir the mixture. If you want your white chocolate chips to maintain their shape in the granola bar, add them after you've combined the almond butter mixture and oat mixture.

Nut-free Trail Mix

Trail mix is a great high-energy snack, but most are loaded with nuts that may not be welcome at your child's school. This delicious mix is super kid friendly and has nutrient-rich pumpkin and sunflower seeds instead of nuts. Most schools allow seeds, but you might want to double check with your child's teacher just to be sure.

Egg whites	1 cup	250 mL
Granulated sugar	2/3 cup	150 mL
Ground cinnamon	1/4 tsp.	1 mL
Ground cloves	1/8 tsp.	0.5 mL
Salt	1/4 tsp.	1 mL
Mini pretzel twists	2 cups	500 mL
Rice cereal squares	1 cup	250 mL
Dried cranberries	1 cup	250 mL
Pumpkin seeds	3/4 cup	175 mL
Sunflower seeds	1/4 cup	60 mL

Combine first 5 ingredients with a whisk in a large bowl until foamy.

Add remaining 5 ingredients and stir to coat. Spread out evenly on a greased baking sheet. Bake in 300°F (150C) oven for about 30 minutes, turning every 10 minutes, until dry. Let stand on baking sheet until cool. Makes 5 cups (1.25 mL).

Packing the lunch kit: No special instructions needed for this trail mix. Just pack a portion in a regular container.

Cocoa-nuts

In our test kitchen, these nuts practically flew off the baking tray! They were a huge hit with kids and adults alike. This recipe results in coating with a dark chocolate flavour; if your kids prefer a sweeter chocolate, add a little more sugar to the mix. Store these nuts in an airtight container for up to 2 weeks. If your kids school doesn't allow nuts, you could always pack a container of these nuts in the car for an after-school snack.

Brown sugar	2 tbsp.	30 mL
Cocoa powder	2 tbsp.	30 mL
Cooking oil	1 tbsp.	15 mL
Vanilla extract	1 tsp.	5 mL
Raw almonds	1 cup	250 mL
Raw pecans	1 cup	250 mL

Combine first 4 ingredients in a medium bowl.

Add almonds and pecans and stir until nuts are well coated. Spread nuts in a single layer on a baking sheet. Bake in 300°F (150°C) degree oven for 10 minutes. Stir and flip nuts with a spatula, breaking up any lumps. Bake about 10 minutes more, until nuts are fragrant. Set aside to cool completely. Makes 2 cups (500 mL) nuts.

Packing the lunch kit: No special instructions needed for these nuts. Just pack them in a regular container.

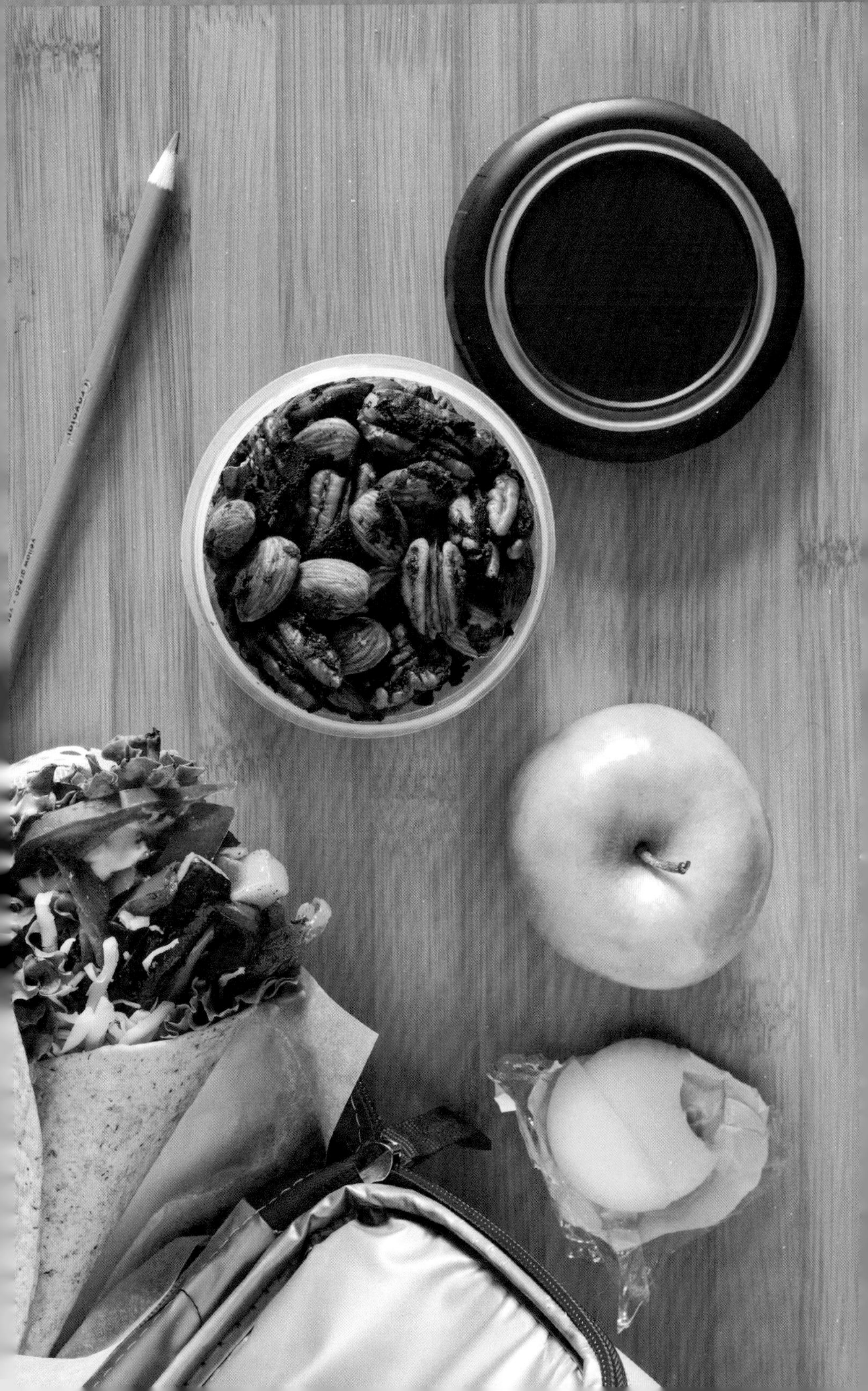

Crispy Chickpeas

Roasted chickpeas make a perfect snack. Kids love them because they are crunchy and fun to eat. You'll love them because they are loaded with nutrients, protein and fibre to keep your kids satisfied until their next meal. And they taste great! Store any leftovers in an airtight container in the fridge for up to 5 days.

Olive oil	2 tbsp.	30 mL
Smoked paprika	1 tsp.	5 mL
Cumin	1/4 tsp.	1 mL
Salt	1/4 tsp.	1 mL
Pepper	1/4 tsp.	1 mL
Can of chickpeas (540 ml, 19 oz.), drained, rinsed and dried (see Tip, below)	1	1

Combine first 5 ingredients in a medium bowl.

Add chickpeas and toss until well coated. Transfer chickpeas to a greased large baking sheet with sides. Bake in 450°F (230°C) oven for 22 to 25 minutes or until crispy, turning half way through. Remove from oven and let cool completely. Makes 8 servings.

Tip: Make sure the chickpeas are extremely dry before you put them in the oven or they will steam instead of crisp up when you bake them. For best results, remove any excess loose skins that come off the chickpeas as you dry them.

Packing the lunch kit: No special instructions needed for these crispy chickpeas. Just pack them in a regular container.

Date Crispies

Chewy and crispy, these balls are reminiscent of a rice crispy treat, only a much healthier version. Check with your school to make sure sunflower seeds are not on their forbidden list before you pack these treats in your kid's lunch box. Date crispies will keep in the fridge for 3 to 5 days but do not freeze.

Butter (or hard margarine)	1 tbsp.	15 mL
Chopped pitted dates	1/2 cup	125 mL
Granulated sugar	1/4 cup	60 mL
Large egg, lightly beaten	1	1
Crisp rice cereal	1 1/2 cups	375 mL
Salted, roasted sunflower seeds	1/4 cup	60 mL

Melt butter in a small saucepan on medium. Add next 3 ingredients. Cook for about 3 minutes, stirring constantly, until thickened. Remove from heat.

Stir in cereal and sunflower seeds. Let stand for about 10 minutes until cool enough to handle. Shape into 1 inch (2.5 cm) balls (see Tip, below). Makes 18 crispies.

Packing the lunch kit: Pack a portion of crispies into a container and place in an insulated lunch bag with a cooler pack. These treats will fall apart if they get too warm.

Tip: Dampen your hands to prevent the date mixture from sticking to them while you are forming it into balls.

Flavoured Applesauce Cups

Making your own flavoured applesauce cups at home allows you to control the texture (chunky vs. smooth) and sweetness of the finished product. Even better, you can create your own fruit combinations! We've used blackberries for this recipe, but you could substitute with any berry, peaches, mango...the possibilities are endless! Homemade applesauce cups are also better for the environment because you use reusable containers instead of disposable plastic cups. Store these cups in the fridge for 5 to 7 days or freeze in individual cups for 2 to 3 months.

Cooking apples (such as McIntosh or Granny Smith), peeled, cored and cut into large chunks	2 lbs.	900 g
Water	3/4 cup	175 mL
Lemon juice	2 tbsp.	30 mL
Blackberries	3/4 cup	175 mL
Maple syrup	1/4 cup	60 mL

Combine apples, water and lemon juice in a large pot over high heat and bring to a boil. Reduce heat to a simmer and cook for 10 to 12 minutes until apples are beginning to break down, adding more water if necessary.

Stir in blackberries and maple syrup. Cook for 5 to 6 minutes until thickened. Remove from heat and mash with a potato masher until you reach your desired consistency. Makes 8 servings.

Packing the lunch kit: Transfer a portion of applesauce to a leakproof container and place it in an insulated lunch bag with a cooler pack.

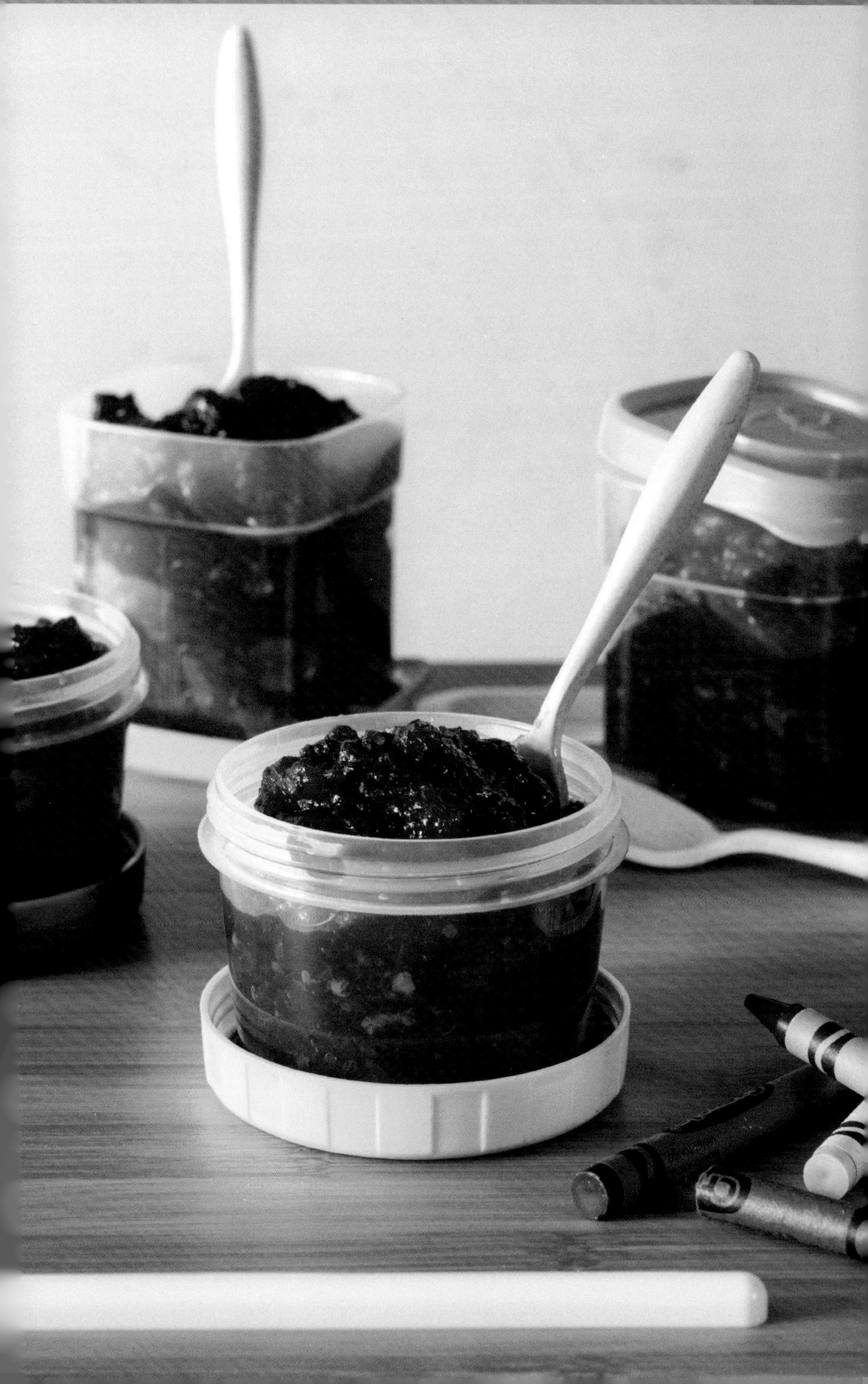

Index

Make-ahead Lunches for Kids

Paré • Pirk • Billey • Darcy

Distributed by
Canada Book Distributors
www.canadabookdistributors.com
www.companyscoming.com
Tel: 1-800-661-9017

Library and Archives Canada Cataloguing in Publication

Title: Make-ahead lunches for kids / Paré, Pirk, Billey, Darcy.
Other titles: Company's Coming
Names: Paré, Jean, 1927- author. | Pirk, Wendy, 1973- author. | Billey, Ashley, author. | Darcy, James, 1956- author.
Identifiers: Canadiana 20190119977 | ISBN 9781772070576 (softcover)
Subjects: LCSH: Lunchbox cooking. | LCSH: School children—Food. | LCSH: Quick and easy cooking. | LCGFT: Cookbooks.
Classification: LCC TX735 .P37 2019 | DDC 641.53083/4—dc23

Cover: jinseiphoto; Ihor Smishko/GettyImages; Tatiana Atamaniuk/GettyImages

All inside photos by jinseiphoto except: from Company's Coming: 93, 105, 115, 133. From gettyimages: anandaBGD, 143; AnastasiaNurullina, 121; Anna1311, 11b; Anna_Shepulova, 89; Bartosz Luczak, 16, 33, 47; bhofack2, 11a, 85; cobraphoto, 131; debbiehelbing, 145; Dzevoniia, 153; Erba Cesare, 41; evgenyatamanenko, 8; Fascinadora, 111; gvictoria, 49; hollydc, 6; LauriPatterson, 129; La–vanda, 10b; Liudmyla Chuhunova, 147; martinrlee, 107; master1305, 45; mukhina1, 5; nata_vkusidey, 10a, 57, 101; pikepicture, 7a-e; Premyuda Yospim, 137; Seagull_I, 51; Tanya_F, 91; Tatiana Atamaniuk, 17, 35; ThitareeSarmkasat, 10c.

A special thanks to Audrey Chan and Jesse Pirk for being the amazing hand models in these photos. Well done, guys!

We acknowledge the financial support of the Government of Canada.
Nous reconnaissons l'appui financier du gouvernement du Canada.

Funded by the Government of Canada
Financé par le gouvernement du Canada | Canadä

PC: 38-1

Table of Contents

The Jean Paré Story

Jean Paré (pronounced "jeen PAIR-ee") grew up understanding that the combination of family, friends and home cooking is the best recipe for a good life. When Jean left home, she took with her a love of cooking, many family recipes and an intriguing desire to read cookbooks as if they were novels!

"Never share a recipe you wouldn't use yourself."

When her four children had all reached school age, Jean volunteered to cater the 50th anniversary celebration of the Vermilion School of Agriculture, now Lakeland College, in Alberta, Canada. Working from her home, Jean prepared a dinner for more than 1,000 people and from there launched a flourishing catering operation that continued for more than 18 years.

As requests for her recipes increased, Jean was often asked, "Why don't you write a cookbook?" The release of *150 Delicious Squares* on April 14, 1981, marked the debut of what would soon turn into one of the world's most popular cookbook series.

Company's Coming cookbooks are distributed in Canada, the United States, Australia and other world markets. Bestsellers many times over in English, Company's Coming cookbooks have also been published in French and Spanish.

Familiar and trusted in home kitchens around the world, Company's Coming cookbooks are offered in a variety of formats. Highly regarded as kitchen workbooks, the softcover Original Series, with its lay-flat plastic comb binding, is still a favourite among home cooks.

Jean Paré's approach to cooking has always called for quick and easy recipes using everyday ingredients. That view served her well, and the tradition continues in the Practical Gourmet series.

Jean's Golden Rule of Cooking is: Never share a recipe you wouldn't use yourself. It's an approach that has worked—millions of times over!

Introduction

Making kids' lunches can be a thankless task. No one wants the same boring sandwich every day, but trying to come up with enticing, nutritious lunches your kids will actually eat can be a real challenge. Finding the time to prepare said enticing, nutritious lunches can be even more so. But it doesn't have to be. With a little advance planning and a few clever shortcuts, you can churn out delicious lunches that will please your kids and make them the envy of their classmates.

What makes a good lunch?

We will not go into the science of nutrition here, but it is safe to say that a balanced lunch includes a source of protein (from lean meats, beans or nuts, if your school allows them), complex carbohydrates (preferably whole grains) and some fruit and veggies. And if you can sneak in a source of calcium (perhaps yogurt or cheese), even better. Think fresh, whole foods and keep the highly processed foods out of the lunchbox or save them for a special treat.

And do leave room for the occasional sweet treat. A sweet surprise in his lunch kit can really make a kid's day, but be choosy about what kind of sweet treat you provide. A highly processed, sugar-laden treat might make your child's taste buds happy, but it could be setting her up for the dreaded mid-afternoon slump. Opt instead for healthier choices that are made with nutritious ingredients and a reasonable amount of fat and sugar. Even better, choose homemade treats so you can control exactly what goes into them. Homemade pudding or whole-grain granola bars, cookies or muffins rival anything you can buy at the store and will still put a smile on your child's face without setting her up for the crash that inevitably follows a sugar rush.

Planning Ahead

So, how do you find the time to prepare these shining examples of mid-day nutrition? In the interest of simplifying your lunch preparation experience, your new mantra will be "cook once, eat many times."

With today's hectic pace, batch cooking can be a real lifesaver for busy parents. Set aside a parcel of time dedicated to filling your fridge and freezer with foods that keep well and can be used to create many different meals. Meatballs, burger patties, chili, soups, pasta sauces, pancakes, waffles…the possibilities are endless. Freeze soups, pasta sauces, chilis and the like in single serving containers. For meatballs, burgers, falafel, waffles and anything else that will stick together and freeze into a solid mound, spread them out in a single layer on baking trays and freeze until firm. Transfer them to resealable freezer bags or containers so you can take out only what you need. Remember to label and date each bag/container. When you have a freezer full of batch-cooked basics to draw from, preparing a nutritious, tasty lunch is a breeze.

Planning for leftovers is another great way to make sure you have easy lunch options for the next day. Make a little extra pasta and salad at supper and pack a portion of each into single-serving containers for everyone's lunch the next day.

If your child balks at the idea of leftovers, dress them up. Last night's chili makes a great topping for today's taco salad or chili dog. Repurposing leftovers breathes new life into the food and keeps things interesting for your kids. If kids are excited about their lunch, they are more likely to eat it.